D1176795

# the conspirators: 20th July 1944

**Roger Manvell**

Editor-in-Chief: Barrie Pitt
Editor: David Mason
Art Director: Sarah Kingham
Picture Editor: Robert Hunt
Designer: David Allen
Cover: Denis Piper
Special Drawings: John Batchelor
Photographic Research: Benedict Shephard
Cartographer: Richard Natkiel

First Printing: April 1971
Printed in United States of America

Ballantine Books Inc.
101 Fifth Avenue New York NY 10003

An Intext Publisher

# Contents

# A murder story

## Introduction by Alan Wykes

Regrettable though it may be, there is a grim satisfaction in watching the plotting of a murder, whether the crime is planned by an individual or a group of conspirators. In fiction or in fact the details exercise our fascination. However ignoble the cause, we trace the effect with pleasure, admiring the assassins' ingenuity or feeling dismay at their ineptitude, as the case may be. In theatre or cinema there is an irrepressible impulse to cry 'Look behind you!' when we are made privy to the wicked designs of baddie upon goodie. In real life we are appalled by the very fact of the murder of a Kennedy or a Martin Luther King; but if some investigator subsequently pieces together the cunning designs of the murderer, shows us his mind – diseased though it may be according to accepted moral standards – and the ingenuity of his machinations, the build-up to the climax is irresistibly exciting. (At least, it is if it is well presented.) Whether we are ultimately moved to horror or approval will depend on innumerable factors, including our sympathies with the murderer's, or conspirators', cause; but it remains fascinating to watch the story unfold.

Adolf Hitler was a man for whom few felt any genuine affection and fewer still any love. He was idolized by millions; but idolatry is not affection: it is merely perverted faith expressed by fawning. Helped by evil minions he attempted to bestride the world like a Colossus but succeeded only in straddling it with the ugly threat of jackboots on his feet and a shabby mind in his head. His mind, like his body, was diseased. It grew besotted with power and it was inevitable that he should become the object of a conspiracy, since it gradually became clearer to less violent characters than his own that he was leading the German nation not to the glory he had promised but to disaster. All of us were, and still are, involved in the outcome of his megalomania.

There were in fact a number of conspiracies to assassinate Hitler and accounts of them are given in the early pages of this book. The ways in which they misfired are themselves interesting and incline one to think that there was some capricious charm attached to Hitler's life. The plot of which all the world learned, however, was planned to take effect on 20th July 1944; and the great merit of Roger Manvell's book is that it not only shows up the steps by which the conspirators mapped out the course of their action, but illuminates them

with a clarity that belies their complexity.

The July Plot also misfired, though not in the literal sense of the planted bomb misfiring. Nor, indeed, because of any weakness in design, and certainly not because of any lack of courage or inattention to detail on the part of Colonel Graf von Stauffenberg, the man designated to plant the bomb in the map room at Rastenburg. One can only say, without much originality, that it failed because fate decided so. Hitler was destined to die by his own hand, not by that of an assassin.

The plot, though, had by no means worked itself out when Stauffenberg mistakenly assumed that it had been successful and passed the word to his fellow conspirators, who were waiting to take control of Government and military forces. The subsequent events as the conspirators tried to stage a *coup d'etat* have about them something of the nature of farce, but of farce perilously balanced on the brink of tragedy. Mysterious phone calls, conversations at cross-purposes, and melodramatic suicides were all part of the aftermath, as were the most horrifying tortures and retributive sentences on the conspirators. There were also those who 'came of their own accord in the hope that by reporting ostensibly to help with the investigations they might be held to have cleared themselves of implication in the conspiracy'.

Though the Resistance movement in Germany was never powerful enough, in practical terms, to amount to a force that could overthrow the Nazi régime – mainly because of the fear of the limitless power of that organization without which no dictatorship can hold its authority, the Secret Police – there was, throughout the ascendant days of Nazism, a strong body of opposition to Hitler and his methods. The opponents included the outspokenly brave and saintly, such as the pastors Niemöller and Bonhoeffer, whose appeal was, hopelessly, to moral values; and those who actively but secretly conspired to bring about the Führer's literal fall by assassination. The July Plotters were of course of this kind. Some of them were partially motivated by self-interest; but without exception they saw in Hitler's mad schemes for world domination the end of Germany. Their heroism, or treachery – according to the viewpoint – makes a gripping story.

# Traitors or national heroes?

Hitler and the ancient President
Hindenburg in Berlin, May 1933

8

Are men traitors to their country if they set out to kill its elected head of state?

Adolf Hitler became Germany's 'legitimate' Chancellor in 1933. He had, as he had always intended since the failure of his abortive local *coup d'état* in Munich in 1923, proceeded to power along a path which at least bore the mask of legitimacy. His Party, which in 1928 gained only 810,000 votes in the election for the Reichstag (that is, the German Federal Parliament of the day), polled nearly 6.5 million in 1930, and over 13.7 million in the July 1932 election, which represented 37 per cent of the votes cast. The Party lost two million of these votes in the last truly free election in pre-Hitler Germany, that of November 1932, representing thirty-three per cent of the voting. It is true that in the March elections of 1933, five weeks after Hitler had been made Chancellor, the votes for the Reichstag were 17.27 million, or forty-three per cent of the voters, but this election was to a considerable extent 'bent' owing to the wholesale arrests of the Communists following the Reichstag fire (for which the Nazis were almost certainly responsible), and the consequent intimidation which the Nazi agents and storm-troopers had been able to bring to bear against their opponents' supporters, including the Social Democrats. Whether in fact the Nazis were responsible for this fire remains a subject of debate even to this day, with eminent historians supporting the idea that the young Dutch incendiarist Marinus van der Lubbe, discovered half-naked in the burning building, was wholly responsible. (For the counter-argument, with new evidence, see Manvell and Fraenkel, *Hermann Göring* (1962) pp 380-82; New English Library Mentor paperback (1968 pp 282-83.) With Hindenburg still President, Hitler seized absolute power under the very noses of the German people, whether they were for him or against him in the first place.

At the time of the seizure of power in 1933, Hitler was forty-four, Göring thirty-nine, Goebbels thirty-six, and Himmler, still very much in the background, only thirty-three. Perhaps because the Nazi *coup d'état* in Germany was, in a sense, a young revolutionary movement, or perhaps because the Nazi leaders were, socially considered, merely upstarts, the first attempts at organized resistance came from the political Right, from men who held themselves to be, first and foremost, officers and gentlemen, and who did not like to see the uniformed services pandering to an agitator who had never risen higher than the rank of corporal in the German army. This is not to belittle the noble discontent among the tens of thousands of Germans (mostly working-class) who were openly opposed to Hitler's flow of arbitrary decrees and regulations following the passing of the Enabling Act of March 1933, which was rushed through the Reichstag Parliament from which his key opponents had been virtually excluded, and which gave him his dictatorial powers. Most of these individuals, representing sporadic resistance which was purely individual, ended up in concentration camps and, if they survived at all, were rendered ineffectual; such were the youthful Hans and Sophie Scholl who in 1942 attempted to establish resistance among the university students, but who were (as we shall see) caught and executed. Nor must the distinguished protesters whom the Nazis dare not imprison be forgotten – in particular those most courageous clerics, Bishop Count von Galen and the Cardinal Archbishop Michael Faulhaber, who openly preached against Hitler and his works. What we are concerned with is the formation of an active group of conspirators who, at various times and in various ways, came together to plan the overthrow, and finally the assassination, of the chosen leader of their country.

What was needed was some central

point, in influential circles, round which resistance could cohere. No individual can conduct a *coup d'état* by himself. It is not sufficient merely to remove the leader, whoever he may be; the ground must be adequately prepared in the Armed Services and the civil administration for the take-over of power to be accepted as a *fait accompli* in the country as a whole. An inner circle of trusted men, each with his appointed task, must gradually and secretly be sworn in; a shadow administration must be prepared to take control of the established services, both military and civil; propaganda must be ready to saturate the broadcasting networks and the press within minutes of the dictator's fall. Conspiracy is no task for amateurs, though amateurs are often enough involved in it, which is one of the principal reasons why so many attempted *coups d'état* fail.

The central point of resistance in Germany was to remain within the

*Above:* Hans, brother of Sophie Scholl. killed by the Gestapo. *Below:* Sophie Scholl, schoolgirl leader of the White Rose Movement. *Right above:* Röhm, principal victim of the Night of the Long Knives. *Right below:* Nazi propaganda display, 1934

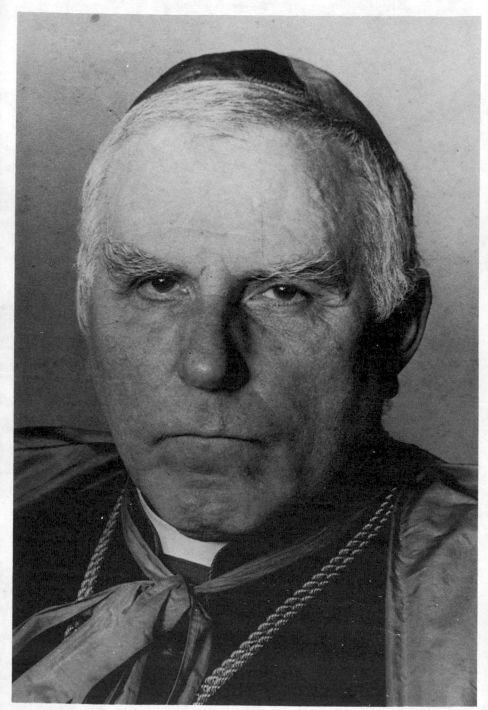

Cardinal von Galen, Bishop of Munster and leading opponent of Hitler

Cardinal Faulhaber, who preached against Nazi policies

*Above:* The Army takes the oath of loyalty to Hitler, August 1934. *Below:* Horse artillery parading for General Fritsch, Potsdam 1934. *Right:* Heavy machine gun team in training 1937

Army throughout the twelve years of the Nazi regime. The rapid infiltration of Party control into the civil administration during 1933–34, and particularly the establishment of a political secret police – the Gestapo – for the purpose of destroying any opposition to the regime, made effective, organized resistance among the civilian population extremely difficult, if not impossible, though naturally anyone could sacrifice his liberty, and perhaps his life, if he chose openly to oppose Hitler. The Army, therefore, remained the only fully armed power within the State which, independent of Hitler, the Führer, could, if resolutely led, have overthrown him. This was the reason why, having established his control over civilian Germany, he turned his attention during the key period of 1934–38 to achieving his personal ascendency in the Army.

He started with certain advantages. He was opposed to communism, and so was the Army. He had come to power with the support of the right-wing Nationalists – and this, broadly speaking, represented the point of view of the officer cadre. When, in 1934, Hitler drew the teeth of his own Party forces, the three million strong stormtroopers, the S A , and murdered their Commandant, his old friend Ernst Röhm, he was able to represent that he had done so because of Röhm's plans to stage his own *coup* and seize command of the Army himself. This preventive measure was completed by Hitler by July 1934. Hitler therefore, in the early days of his rule, was as careful to foster his good relations with the Army as he had been much earlier to woo the German industrialists. He was, so to speak, their man in politics – ready to re-establish conscription in defiance of the Versailles treaty, and restore the German Army to its former prestige in the Fatherland.

But if Hitler set himself up to be their man, he was equally determined to see that they were his. Immediately on the death of President Hindenburg in August 1934, he created himself not only Head of State but also Supreme Commander-in-Chief of the Armed Forces of the Reich. The offices of President and Chancellor were abolished as obsolete. Hitler was to be all in all for the civilian and serviceman alike. Without any prior warning, every man in uniform had to swear his personal oath of allegiance to him:

'I swear by God this holy oath: I will render unconditional obedience to the Führer of the German Reich and People, Adolf Hitler, the Supreme Commander of the Armed Forces, and will be ready, as a brave soldier, to stake my life at any time to this oath.'

Men in uniform are peculiarly susceptible to the mystique of loyalty, and this oath and its magic were to prove a constant deterrent to the establishment of a widespread resistance movement in the one area of the Reich where it could be most effectively developed – the Armed Services.

The oath of allegiance meant that any man in uniform who became involved in a plot to secure Hitler's downfall was a traitor in a double sense – he was betraying his Fatherland's appointed leader, and he was betraying Hitler in person. Those who were eventually to join the inner circle of conspirators did so because they were convinced that Hitler's virtually illegal seizure of power was in itself a greater act of treason than anything they, the enforced bearers of this oath, might perpetrate in seeking his removal, whether by arrest or by assassination.

The organized opposition to Hitler was to become a tragic operation, with two succeeding objectives, first,

to arrest the Führer and put him on trial as a traitor, and secondly, when the war was in progress and Germany's position had become more morally desperate, to remove him and his associates by assassination and effect a *coup d'état*. The many reasons why this active opposition never succeeded is the story we have to tell. It came very close indeed to success both in March 1943 and in July 1944, and failed in this last instance only through sheer misfortune and what proved to be in certain respects wholly inadequate planning. But behind this too lay the flaws in human nature, flaws due to differences in background, age group, class and political outlook, as well as to a certain innocence of mind and lack of that kind of utter ruthlessness which carries an action through to success in spite of its apparent impossibility. The cards seemed stacked for success in July 1944, and several heroic men were prepared to wager their lives upon this final throw, and so paid the price of their failure. It was, in its way, a human and political tragedy of a kind which could have attracted the interest of Shakespeare. Indeed, the July plot of 1944 has certain affiliations with *Julius Caesar*, though in this instance the *coup* failed after the dictator had fallen, whereas in the case of the July plot the dictator survived by a miracle, and so lived to exact a fearful revenge on his opponents.

It was left then to the Allied Forces to drive Hitler to suicide some ten months later. Meanwhile a great host of men, women and children were to die – in the devastation of war and bombing, and in the massacre of the concentration camps – human beings who might have survived had Stauffenberg's bomb not been inadvertently moved from under Hitler's feet. Such are the accidents of history.

# Resistance — the first generation

Goebbels (centre) with Himmler (left)
and Admiral Canaris (right)

Wilhelm Canaris, newly created an Admiral, became head of German Military Intelligence (the Abwehr) in January 1935. At forty-seven, he had thought he was on his way towards retirement, but his extraordinary character, and the peculiar nature of his past activities, combined to make him well suited in the eyes of his seniors to fulfil a difficult and delicate task which involved understanding the requirements of the Armed Services while at the same time keeping a reasonable relationship with the Party's Intelligence – in this case, the secret police and the SD, the Intelligence department of Himmler's SS, headed by the formidable young former naval officer, Reinhard Heydrich, whom Canaris had known in the Service during the early 1920s. Canaris's wife, Erika, enjoyed playing the violin, and Heydrich, equally musical, had, as a naval lieutenant, been happy to bring his violin to Canaris's house to help make up Erika's string quartets.

Canaris was a man of some culture, but of a secretive nature; he had worked during the first world war in Naval Intelligence. He was a strange man – volatile, charming, introspective and given to melancholy. He was also a romantic, who liked to let people believe he was of Greek origin, and whose favourite haunts were always to be in the Mediterranean; the sunshine soothed him. He was in many respects brilliant, a good linguist with a quick brain when it came to anticipating and avoiding difficulties. A career man in the Navy, he had served with some distinction on the *Dresden* during the celebrated action off the Falkland Islands, parleying with the British when the *Kent* and *Glasgow* finally cornered the German cruiser off the Chilean coast. When the *Dresden* was scuttled and the crew interned, Canaris had eventually escaped and made his way back to Europe, where he had served as a spy in Spain and Italy. Later he had commanded a submarine in Mediter-

ranean waters. After the war, he was involved in various right-wing political activities, including the Kapp Putsch against the Weimar Republic, but he finally became a staff officer in the Navy, with every sign that the adventures of his professional life were now over.

As he sat at his modest desk in the Abwehr office in 1935 in Berlin, he looked, as indeed he was, unassuming, benevolent and rubicund. Everything about him was small, his height, his feet, his hands. Those who knew him best realized he was insatiably curious, an excellent listener and a good judge of character. He needed to be, for he was to turn the inner core of his organization known as the Central Office, or more simply as department Z, into a centre for disaffection.

In this he was first encouraged by his second-in-command, an Army officer called Hans Oster. Oster, who was forty, was the very opposite of Canaris – talkative where Canaris was taciturn, rash where he was discrete, a man of action where Canaris was more of an intellectual. Oster was in many respects a typical man of the world; he had recently suffered temporary dismissal from the Army on account of a love affair he had enjoyed with the wife of a senior officer. He liked to refer to Hitler as 'Emil', and regarded this as sufficient cover to say what he liked about him. But Oster was an open and honest man, thin, pale, handsome, elegant, and above all courageous. Canaris liked him, and from the first they formed a close association. Both were right-wing nationalists in politics, but they agreed that, whatever their opinions of Hitler had been in the past, they could not wait now to see him removed. If anything, Oster's views on Hitler had hardened before those of Canaris.

Canaris, however, was nothing if not circumspect. His job was to provide an Intelligence service in effect for all the armed services, and with the rapid growth of the Army while

Hitler's plans for aggression were maturing, the strength of Canaris's department expanded proportionately. Canaris and Oster determined, however, to create a small, inner circle of like-minded men who were to form the nucleus of disaffection against Hitler, while at the same time carrying on their normal Intelligence duties. Only a minute percentage of men in the service of the Abwehr were ever to know what their senior officers were planning. At the same time, Canaris revived his ostensible friendship with Heydrich, whom he realized was the most dangerous man in the State so far as he was concerned. Soon Heydrich's violin was to be heard again in the comfortable precincts of Canaris's new house in Dahlem, a select suburb of Berlin. The Admiral, as head of military Intelligence, was watching Heydrich, while Heydrich, as head of SS Intelligence, was watching Canaris.

It has been said that Canaris, like so many others, was secretly frightened of Heydrich, whose ice-cold brain and cynical ruthlessness was in such marked contrast to Himmler's diffidence when it came to decisive action. Heydrich was to be Himmler's chief executive when it came to carrying out the initial phases of the genocide programme of the 1940s. Meanwhile he was engaged in humbler tasks; he gave Werner Best, the SS lawyer who was later to be put in charge of occupied Denmark, the responsibility for sorting out the various fields of interest as between the Abwehr and SD Intelligence. In a special memorandum composed for the author and his colleague Heinrich Fraenkel when writing the biographical study of Himmler, which they published in 1965, Werner Best has described the process:

'Canaris was very methodical, very much an organizer building up a vast machinery which, in the end, employed

Heydrich (left) at practice with SS comrades. He was an outstanding fencer

many more civil servants than it did agents or spies. It was not too difficult to segregate the respective spheres of action - such as active military espionage for the Army and criminal investigation for the Police. Much more difficult - in fact practically impossible - was the division of responsibilities in the field of counter-espionage, even though we had agreed in principle that tracing foreign espionage was a matter for the Abwehr (if only because Police Intelligence had insufficient agents for this) . . . There should have been constant collaboration and mutual confidence between the Abwehr and Police Intelligence, but personal rivalries and problems of prestige frequently got the better of us.'

Both departments in fact grew to considerable proportions during the years preceding the war.

Canaris and Oster soon began to discover, both inside and outside the Army, men in influential places whom they might trust. Closest to them was a man everyone liked and respected, General Ludwig Beck, Chief of the Army General Staff since 1933. When Canaris took over the Abwehr, Beck was aged fifty-five. He was a brilliant career officer of the old school, a student of military history, an intellectual who was also a kindly and considerate gentleman, noted for his high integrity and his right-wing views. But with all these attributes, he was not cut out to be a leader in any kind of action; he was not a man to make quick, intuitive decisions, and his health was failing. He, like the rest in the Army, found he was suddenly required to take the personal oath of loyalty to Hitler. 'This is the blackest day of my life,' he said afterwards.

In his key position in the High Command, he soon discovered that plans had only one purpose - to prepare Germany to wage an aggressive war. It was for this conscription had been introduced, for this rearmament pressed forward, for this the

23

nation's economy made so stringent. Beck, small, frail, but eloquent, dared to oppose this policy to Hitler's face. Naturally, Beck was rigidly opposed to Communism, but he soon found that he could not tolerate Hitler's methods of challenging it with an equally inflexible militarism.

In the gradual forging of the links of opposition to Hitler in the higher echelons of right-wing German society, the men without uniforms were to be almost as important as those with them. From the diplomatic corps came another highly-principled ally, Ulrich von Hassell, Germany's ambassador to Rome, and son-in-law of the distinguished Grand-Admiral von Tirpitz. In 1938, when Ribbentrop became Hitler's Foreign Minister after serving as his ambassador in Britain, Hassell was suddenly retired and left in Berlin without any further employment. As ambassador, he had had to take part in the negotiations for the Rome-Berlin axis, which was signed in November 1936. He saw this quite plainly as another link in the chain leading to war in Europe.

His house, like that of Beck, became a centre from 1938 where men of like mind could talk freely. Hassell, who in 1938 was fifty-seven, certainly looked the aristocrat – he was lean-faced with a close-clipped moustache. In spite of his dismissal, he retained his diplomatic status and, like Beck, was a man people of his own kind in society liked. He had little to do, apart from holding a useful sinecure position attached to the Board of the Central European Economic Conference through which he gained a great deal of useful information. He began to keep a secret diary which, when the days grew darker, his wife was to hide in a tea-chest buried in their garden; this diary gives an almost day-to-day account from the autumn of 1938 of how Hassell's many discussions on behalf of the resistance progressed, with their frustrating ups and downs. He was a man of high courage but, like Beck, not a true conspirator. It soon began to be evident that what the German resistance needed was an able buccaneer, not scholars or diplomats like Beck and Hassell, or elaborately wary customers like Canaris.

Dr Carl Goerdeler was, perhaps, a step in the direction towards introducing a buccaneer into the Resistance. He was another conservative nationalist, trained in law, and with a career in municipal administration. He came of a distinguished Prussian family. In 1933, Hitler's year of triumph, he was mayor of Leipzig, which in Germany is a paid appointment in civil administration. At first he had approved of Hitler's policy, as he understood it, sufficiently to offer him his active support as an economic adviser. Goerdeler was a man of extremes, brilliant, volatile, emotional and lacking circumspection. He would fly off the handle over anything of which he violently disapproved – and it is typical of him that he resigned his position as mayor of Leipzig when, against his express orders, the Party authorities removed the statue of Mendelssohn from its public place in Leipzig, the city where this Jewish composer was born. His anti-Nazi views now boiled over. He took a cover-job as representative of the firm of Bosch, and in 1938 began his peripatetic life as self-appointed roving ambassador for the Resistance, travelling alike in Germany and abroad, and making his fellow members of the Resistance shudder at the open indiscretion of his remarks about Hitler. He was also certainly planning the future of Germany when Hitler was gone – its administration, its economy. Perhaps he was a little mad. He was certainly as unwise as he was courageous. In 1938 he was fifty-two, and so belonged to the same age-group as the others, whom he came to know well, more especially Hassell.

These, then, were the key men

**Hans Oster, one of the earliest military conspirators against Hitler**

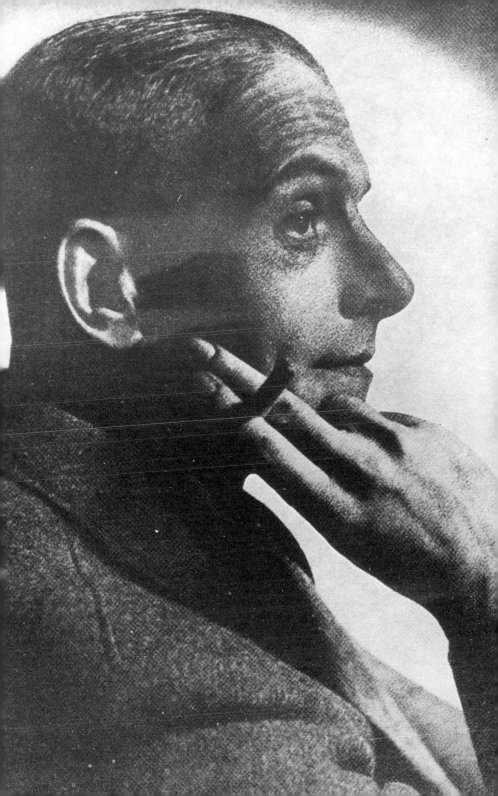

**Ludwig Beck, Chief of the Army General Staff until 1938**

working towards organized resistance to Hitler in 1938, and only one of them held a position of real authority – General Beck. But soon he was to resign (in August 1938) after the notorious Blomberg and Fritsch cases, in which the unscrupulous practices of Hitler and his colleagues were to be openly revealed to those near enough to the top to know what was happening. With Beck living in retirement, only Canaris was left in a position of influence, as distinct from actual executive authority in the Army. This was considerably to weaken the powers of the Resistance.

But it was the Blomberg and Fritsch affairs which brought the resolution of those opposed to Hitler to the point of promoting their first deliberate action against him. Field-Marshal Werner von Blomberg was Minister of War and Commander-in-Chief of the Armed Forces. In January 1938, after seeking Göring's private advice, he married a young woman with whom he was infatuated. Göring accepted this somewhat humiliating situation with alacrity because he evidently recognized in it a weak point in Blomberg's armour. A general of the old school in the High Command, Blomberg was as opposed to Hitler's get-war-quick methods as he was incapable of carrying them out, and Göring saw in the marriage a means of ridding Hitler of this incubus at the top of the High Command without going to the lengths of offending the Army hierarchy by dismissing him for incompetence. Göring soon discovered that the girl who so fascinated Blomberg at the age of sixty had once been a prostitute – though whether the enquiries into her past preceded or succeeded the marriage, at which both Hitler and Göring acted as witnesses, is open to question. Suffice it to say that while Blomberg was disporting himself with his new wife on Capri, Oster was sent south with the terms of Blomberg's dismissal from his appointments on the grounds that he had disgraced himself, the Armed Services,

and the Führer. It was, after all, unthinkable that Hitler should have been invited to act as witness at the wedding of a prostitute. Blomberg was most conveniently finished.

At the very time Hitler was ridding himself of the unwanted Blomberg, the next in line for the appointment, General Werner von Fritsch, Commander-in-Chief of the German Army, was about to be 'framed' on charges of homosexuality. Hitler no more wanted the services of Fritsch than those of Blomberg; but above all, he wanted the High Command put in its place – and the best way to do this was to stun them by suddenly producing 'evidence', such as these two cases were supposed so melodramatically to reveal, of the corruption in their midst. But he reckoned without the extraordinary *esprit de corps* of these high-placed officers. Just before Fritsch was summoned into Hitler's presence to be confronted by the Gestapo's disreputable witness, Hans Schmidt, who made a living by blackmailing homosexuals, he was secretly prewarned by one of Hitler's adjutants, so that he could prepare himself for this confrontation. He did so with dignity and contempt. Beck, acting for the General Staff as a whole, insisted that a full Court of Enquiry should be set up to examine the nature of the evidence; they all believed Fritsch to be innocent. This placed Hitler and the Gestapo in a dilemma, because it was unlikely Hans Schmidt, whom the Gestapo had merely intimidated into blurting out lies in Hitler's presence, could stand up to cross-examination in the stringent conditions of a Court of Enquiry.

Hitler had to act fast. The Court of Enquiry was set for 10th March. During February Hitler arbitrarily abolished the post of Minister for War, dismissed sixteen generals from the Staff, and appointed himself Commander-in-Chief of the Armed Forces in succession to Blomberg; this served to consolidate his hold on the Army of which he was already

*Above:* Uneasy tablemates: Canaris and Heydrich, heads of the rival intelligence services. *Below:* Dr Werner Best (third from right)

Supreme Commander. Fritsch, suspended from duty pending the enquiry, was also summarily replaced by Field-Marshal Walther von Brauchitsch, a man Hitler knew would have neither the will nor the strength to oppose him.

On 10th March the Court of Enquiry met under the presidency of Göring. The Army was prepared for a showdown with the Gestapo, which technically had no jurisdiction over men in the uniformed services, as distinct from the civilian population. The evidence was that the Gestapo had framed the case under pressure from Himmler and Heydrich. Himmler, indeed, was known to be on tenterhooks about the outcome; according to his aide, Walther Schellenberg, later to become successor to Heydrich as head of SS Intelligence, he even sought to bring telepathic influence to bear on the court whilst it was in session. This move was unlikely to meet with much success, since the four assessors for the Court were Oster, Dr Carl Sack, Chief of the Army Judiciary, and, acting for the Ministry of Justice, the Count von der Goltz and a brilliant young lawyer, Dr Hans von Dohnanyi, son of the composer. Dohnanyi was later to play an heroic part in the Resistance.

Göring, of course, knew what was in the wind, and accordingly appointed himself president of the Court. The date, too, was fortuitous; on 11th March, the day following, the Austrian *Anschluss* was announced, and the Army immediately involved in the 'peaceful' take-over of Austria. The Court had hastily to be postponed, and was only re-convened on 17th March, when Hitler's prestige was at its height, and Göring could afford summarily to dismiss the hearing without considering the Army's evidence against the Gestapo, since Schmidt the blackmailer had been led to admit that he was mistaken in identifying the General. The man he had been blackmailing was an officer called *Frisch*. Göring seized on this

admission, which was all that was needed to clear Fritsch's name, and the Court was dismissed. But Fritsch, his position in the High Command already disposed of, never recovered from this affront to his dignity. He did not seek reinstatement. When, the following year, Poland was invaded, he deliberately sought death while on active service in the regiment in which he held the rank of honorary colonel.

But the Court of Enquiry had a further outcome. It united Canaris and Oster with Dohnanyi, and so won them a colleague as able as he was loyal to the cause of the German Resistance.

By early in January 1938, the meetings were being held which connected Canaris, Oster, and later Dohnanyi, on the one hand, with Goerdeler, Hassell and Beck on the other. Beck was still a member of the High Command, and knew well enough what Hitler was attempting to drive into the heads of his generals.

It was at this stage that a succession of missions to Britain began – all of them modest, individual attempts to warn influential people which way Hitler's plans were moving. Goerdeler, for example, was in Britain in July 1938, and achieved a meeting with Sir Robert Vansittart, Chief Diplomatic Adviser to the British Government. Most of these missions of warning, however, were to take place the following year, 1939.

Another of Hitler's defecting officials was Hjalmar Schacht, former President of the Reichsbank and Minister for Economic Affairs. He had finally left his Ministry in December 1937 because Hitler had appointed Göring, over Schacht's head, as Plenipotentiary for the Five Year Economic Plan. Göring was the last person to bother about orthodox methods when it came to national economic planning. Schacht, nominally at least, swung over to the Resistance through Beck, though he was never to be very helpful. But he was a further influen-

*Left:* Von Hassel, German ambassador to Rome, with Mussolini's son-in-law.
*Above:* Generals Brauchitsch (front) Fromm (left), Beck (centre), Witzleben (right)

tial name to conjure with in the background. Close to Schacht was a young man called Hans Bernd Gisevius, who was to join the Resistance as a most useful go-between, linking the various disparate wings from which the Resistance was finally to be made up. He had worked briefly in the Gestapo, the political police, during its early, embryonic days under Göring, and was to pass from one to the other of various departments in the civil service. He had a friend called Arthur Nebe in the Prussian Criminal Police, who was to be a further useful source of information for the Resistance.

Meanwhile, Canaris was becoming increasingly an absentee from his office in Berlin, leaving the more routine administration to Oster. When at home, Canaris felt restless; he

would arrive with his two faithful dachshunds, who stayed with him in the office all day. But he avoided prolonged periods in Berlin; his knowledge of Spanish led Hitler to entrust him with liaison work with Franco; it is perhaps significant that although Hitler helped Franco with arms, men and aircraft during the Spanish Civil War, Franco was never to offer equivalent help to Hitler when he needed it later. This was no doubt due in some measure at least to the restraining influence of Canaris.

Beck, before he finally resigned from his position as Chief of Staff in August 1938, did what he could to induce some resistance to Hitler's aggressive policy among his colleagues in the High Command. The Führer's target in 1938 was Czechoslovakia, and in particular the Sudeten territory, which was primarily occupied by a minority of German origin who, led by Konrad Henlein, were determined to defect to Hitler, bringing the Sudeten territory with them to be added to Greater Germany.

During 1938, the year of Munich, it was Beck's intention to try to inspire Brauchitsch to give some lead, at least, in opposition to Hitler; all Brauchitsch would do was allow Beck to summon a conference of generals of the High Command in August. At this conference, with Hitler safely away in the Berghof, his mountain retreat in the south on the Bavarian-Austrian border, the generals felt freer to agree with the substance of what Beck said, though Brauchitsch failed to add his support. When Hitler heard of this evidence of what he held to be the pusillanimous spirit among his generals, on whom he had to rely for the conduct of his future wars, he summoned them to the Berghof and gave them a severe reprimand together with a lecture on what he considered to be Germany's needs. In the circumstances, Beck felt forced to hand in his resignation on 18th August, and, after addressing his colleagues for the last time on 27th August, left the War Office for good.

Beck's place was taken by General Franz Halder, who was himself by no means unsympathetic to the Resistance, and was also to become a useful diarist. But he was a careful man, precise and wary, and retained his place on the General Staff.

It was now that the first active revolt against Hitler, confined mainly to the Army though with key civilian links, was planned during the tense summer months of 1938 before the Munich agreement was reached. It was described by Gisevius when he was giving evidence at the International Military Tribunal in Nuremberg after the war:

'Beck had assured us at the time of his resignation – by us I mean Goerdeler, Schacht and other politicians – that he would leave to us a successor who was more energetic than himself,

*Below:* Hitler in Leipzig, March 1934. The Burgermeister and resistance figure, Carl Goerdeler is on his left. *Right:* Dr Carl Goerdeler, Burgermeister of Leipzig

*Left:* **General Blomberg, Minister of War.** *Above:* **Hitler, Blomberg and Fritsch, with the English military expert J F C Fuller**

and who was firmly determined to precipitate a revolution if Hitler should decide upon war. That man whom Beck trusted, and to whom he introduced us, was General Halder. As a matter of fact, on taking office General Halder immediately took steps to start discussions on the subject with Schacht, Goerdeler, Oster and our entire group. A few days after he took over his office, he sent for Oster and informed him that he considered that we were drifting towards war, and that he would undertake an overthrow of the government. He asked Oster what he, for his part, intended to do to include the civilians in the plot . . . We were only a small circle at the time, and Oster replied that to the best of his knowledge he only knew two civilians of importance with whom Halder could have preliminary political conversations; one was Goerdeler and the other was Schacht. Halder refused to speak personally to a man as suspect as Goerdeler, because he felt it too dangerous for him to receive a man whom he did not yet know. While he could find some official reason for a conference with Schacht, Halder asked Oster to act as an intermediary in the matter. Through my agency Oster approached Schacht. Schacht was prepared. A private meeting was to be arranged, and I warned Schacht and told him: 'Have Halder come to your apartment so that you are quite sure of the matter.' Halder then visited Schacht personally at the end of July 1938, and informed him that matters had reached a stage when war was imminent, and that he, Halder, would precipitate a *putsch*. He then asked Schacht whether he was prepared to play a leading part in aiding him politically. That is what Schacht told me at the time . . . I continually acted as an intermediary in these discussions.'

Field-Marshal von Brauchitsch

Walter Schellenberg

The plan was quite simply for the more dissident of the generals as a body to arrest Hitler and place him immediately on trial; the charge would be that his activities constituted a grave danger to Germany. It was intended that an important element in the prosecution should be a medical report on Hitler which would show him to be insane. To obtain such a report, Hans von Dohnanyi (who had been asked to help in the preparation of the case for the prosecution) went with his friend, Otto John, another member of the inner Resistance circle, to visit his father-in-law, Professor Karl Bonhoeffer, father of the celebrated Pastor, Dietrich Bonhoeffer, and a most distinguished neurologist, to ask him to endorse the case that Hitler was insane. They gave the Professor a report listing every known illness from which Hitler had suffered, and the Professor admitted that 'from this it would seem very likely that the man is not quite sane.' The Professor, however, was too correct to issue his visitors with an actual medical report on Hitler's insanity, since he was unable to examine the patient in person.

Dohnanyi introduced a younger element into the inner core of the German Resistance. In 1938 he was only thirty-six. He was linked by marriage to the distinguished Bonhoeffer family, having married the Professor's daughter, Christine, in 1925. He was, in 1938, assistant to Franz Gürtner, Hitler's Minister of Justice. Gürtner, though he had supported Hitler in the earlier stages of his career, was now to act as a brake on his worst activities. Dohnanyi was in Gürtner's confidence, but in 1938 he was sent away to become a Judge in the Supreme Court in Leipzig largely because he would not join the Nazi Party. Nevertheless, he was constantly in Berlin, keeping in close touch with Oster and Beck. Canaris meanwhile went off to Hungary to try to prevent the Hungarians making parallel claims to those of Germany on Czechoslovakian territory.

As Hitler's clash with Czechoslovakia developed towards its climax in the summer of 1938, further missions were sent to London under the influence of Beck and his associates. Following in the comparatively ineffective footsteps of Goerdeler, Major Ewald von Kleist-Schmensin, a friend of both Beck and Canaris, went to London, the ground having been pre-

Hans von Dohnanyi

telling him that when it comes to a showdown neither France nor England will do anything.''

What Kleist was anxious to achieve was recognition that unless Hitler was stopped by some real show of resolution by Britain and France, Czechoslovakia (beginning with the Sudetenland) would follow in the wake of Austria. Kleist told Vansittart that Hitler showed every sign of certainty that Britain and France would never take action over Czechoslovakia.

Vansittart described in his official report Kleist's final words on the matter:

'A great part of the country is sick of the present regime and even a part that is not sick of it is terribly alarmed at the prospect of war, and the conditions to which war will lead is unanimous against it if they can get any support. I wish that one of your leading statesmen would make a speech which would appeal to this element in Germany, emphasizing the horrors of war and the inevitable general catastrophe to which it would lead!...' In conclusion he said that his exit from Germany had been facilitated by his friends in the army on whose unanimity he had enlarged earlier and that he had long been on the most intimate terms with them. They had taken the risk and he had taken the risk of coming out of Germany at this crucial moment although he had no illusions as to the fate that awaited him if he failed; but he made it abundantly clear as I have said earlier, that they alone could do nothing without assistance from outside on the lines he had suggested.'

All Chamberlain did, following this report, was to summon to London for consultation Sir Nevile Henderson, Britain's ambassador in Berlin and a notable supporter of the policy of appeasement.

Kleist, however, went on to see Churchill at Chartwell. Churchill, who was not a member of the Chamberlain administration, proved far

pared for him to some extent by Ian Colvin, the Berlin correspondent of the London newspaper The News Chronicle, and Sir George Ogilvie-Forbes of the British Embassy in Berlin.

Kleist left for London in August 1938, and met Vansittart, Lord Lloyd of the Foreign Office, and Winston Churchill. Kleist was received somewhat coolly in official circles in London, meeting Vansittart first of all. Kleist was very frank, as Vansittart reported:

'Herr von Kleist at once opened up with the utmost frankness and gravity. He said (and this coincides with a great deal of other information which I have given you from entirely different sources) that war was now a certainty unless we stopped it. I said, "Do you mean an extreme danger?" He answered, "No, I do not mean an extreme danger, I mean an absolute certainty." I said, "Do you mean to say that the extremists are now carrying Hitler with them?" He said, "No, I do not mean that. There is only one real extremist and that is Hitler himself. He is the great danger and he is doing this entirely on his own. He receives a great deal of encouragement from Herr von Ribbentrop who keeps

*Above:* Hitler enters Vienna after the Anschluss, March 1938. *Below:* Hitler's triumphant return to Berlin from Vienna. *Right:* Austrian soldiers welcomed by Berliners at the Brandenburg Gate

Left: Vansittart (centre) Diplomatic Advisor to the British government and passionate opponent of Nazism with Sir Anthony Eden (left). *Above left:* Schacht, who fell out early with Hitler. *Above right:* Gisevins, the ex-Gestapo official who dabbled in resistance. *Below left:* Arthur Nebe, police official and resistance sympathiser. *Below right:* Karl Bonhoeffer

more forthcoming than the British government, and wrote on 19th August 1938 to Kleist, after the latter's return to Germany:

'I have welcomed you here as one who is ready to run risks to preserve the peace of Europe and to achieve a lasting friendship between the British, French and German peoples for their mutual advantage.

'I am sure that the crossing of the frontier of Czechoslovakia by German armies or aviation in force will bring about a renewal of the world war. I am as certain as I was at the end of July 1914 that England will march with France and certainly the United States is now strongly anti-Nazi. It is difficult for democracies in advance and in cold blood to make precise declarations, but the spectacle of an armed attack by Germany upon a small neighbour and the bloody fighting that will follow will rouse the whole British Empire and compel the gravest decisions.

'Do not, I pray you, be misled upon this point. Such a war, once started, would be fought out like the last to the bitter end, and one must consider not what might happen in the first few months, but where we should all be at the end of the third or fourth year. It would be a great mistake to imagine that the slaughter of the civil population following upon air-raids would prevent the British Empire from developing its full war power; though, of course, we should suffer more at the beginning than we did last time. But the submarine is practically mastered by scientific methods and we shall have the freedom of the seas and the support of the greater part of the world. The worse the air slaughter at the beginning, the more inexpiable would be the war. Evidently, all the great nations engaged in the struggle, once started, would fight on for victory or death.

'As I felt you should have some definite message to take back to your friends in Germany who wish to see peace preserved and who look forward to a great Europe in which England, France and Germany will be working together for the prosperity of the wage-earning masses, I communicated with Lord Halifax. His Lordship asked me to say on his behalf that the position of His Majesty's Government in relation to Czechoslovakia is defined by the Prime Minister's speech in the House of Commons on 24th March, 1938. The speech must be read as a whole, and I have no authority to select any particular sentence out of its context; but I must draw your attention to the final passage on this subject...

'"Where peace and war are concerned, legal obligations are not alone involved, and, if war broke out, it would be unlikely to be confined to those who have assumed such obligations. It would be quite impossible to say where it would end and what Governments would become involved. The inexorable pressure of facts might well prove more powerful than formal pronouncements, and in that event it would be well within the bounds of probability that other countries, besides those which were parties to the original dispute, would almost immediately become involved. This is especially true in the case of two countries like Great Britain and France, with long associations of friendship, with interests closely interwoven, devoted to the same ideals of democratic liberty, and determined to uphold them."

'May I say that, speaking for myself, I believe that a peaceful and friendly solution of the Czechoslovak problem would pave the way for the true reunion of our countries on the basis of the greatness and the freedom of both.'

Other German spokesmen followed who aimed at stiffening British resistance to Hitler's demands; the details may be found in *The Canaris Conspiracy*, Manvell and Fraenkel, p.41.

**Halder, Chief of the Army General Staff, 1938-42**

*Above left:* Franz Gürtner, Nazi Minister of Justice. *Above right:* Ewald von Kleist-Schmensin, who undertook to put the resistance into touch with the British Foreign Office. *Right:* Ribbentrop (left), German Ambassador to London

One of them, Theodor Kordt, a counsellor in the German Embassy in London, actually spoke to Lord Halifax, the Foreign Secretary. But it was September, and Chamberlain was already beginning to make up his mind to fly to Germany and negotiate in person what was to amount to the sell-out of Czechoslovakia. This was to have a catastrophic effect on the shaky morale of the generals who were hovering on the brink of an actual revolt against Hitler.

The more dissident generals who survived the war were always to claim it was Chamberlain who spiked their guns by suddenly announcing that he, Europe's elder statesman, would fly to Germany to negotiate with Hitler, whose period in power still amounted to only five and a half years. It is claimed that Beck (just retired), Halder, his successor, General Erwin von Witzleben (a commander in the Berlin area), Count Wolf Heinrich von Helldorf, President of Police in Berlin, General Erich Hoepner, who commanded the Third Panzer Division south of Berlin, to say nothing of Canaris and Oster, were poised to stage a military *coup* against Hitler

which would give a lead to others in the High Command opposed to his preparations for war. A young man of spirit on the staff of the Abwehr, Friedrich Wilhelm Heinz, was privately ordered by Witzleben at Oster's house in September to form a small commando group of trusted and active men, including civilians, to carry out Hitler's arrest. Even more private arrangements were made, apparently, to ensure that Hitler would be shot during the action. How far these plans for some sudden strike staged at a conference of the High Command would have resulted in success must forever remain in doubt. But there can be no question that at this stage in the history of Hitler's Reich a military *coup d'état* prior to the Munich agreement would have been far more likely to command wide-scale support in Germany than at any time after Munich.

However this may be, the news that Chamberlain was prepared to fly to meet Hitler in Berchtesgaden came as a profound shock to all those planning an action against the Führer. It seemed to them almost like a betrayal after the efforts they had made in

*Above:* Sir Neville Henderson, British Ambassador to Berlin (seated). His companions are Lady Londonderry and Princess Bibescu. *Below:* Churchill, a photograph taken during his years in the wilderness. *Right:* Neville Chamberlain

Britain. Canaris learned the news while dining, and his trusted friend, Colonel Erwin Lahousen, a recruit from Austrian Intelligence, records him as saying of Chamberlain, 'What *he* – visit that man!' Chamberlain had provided exactly the right deterrent to damp down the weakening enthusiasm of the generals to make any real stand against Hitler, of whom they were terrified. So the project was shelved, and the way left clear for the notorious Munich agreement, in which Hitler's demands on Czechoslovakia were met in full. Nobody among the general public in Britain seemed to care a button. Hitler, of course, pursuing his course of bluff, was to claim that the Sudetenland was his last territorial claim in Europe – but this he must have. 'I will smash the Czechs,' he cried to Sir Horace Wilson, who had come to Berlin as Chamberlain's representative.

The deadline was 1st October 1938, and the Czechs appeared to have mobilized a million men, while even Britain and France were mobilizing what men they could muster. Roosevelt, speaking for the United States, voiced a feeble protest to Hitler. It was Mussolini who intervened as arbitrator on 28th September, and Chamberlain, with Daladier, the French Prime Minister, hastened to Munich. On 30th September the Munich Agreement was signed, and on 1st October Hitler's forces entered the Sudetenland. How could one put down so brilliant a strategist as the Führer?

The German people were only too happy to rejoice in such bloodless victories as the Austrian Anschluss and the occupation of the Sudetenland. What they were in general opposed to was outright war, and this showed itself (to Hitler's disgust) when the Führer ordered Witzleben to parade his armies in the streets of Berlin on 27th September, just to show what was in store for the Czechs. Everyone in the German Resistance was staggered by the success of

*Above:* Halifax, Chamberlain's foreign minister. *Right:* Field-Marshal von Witzleben

Hitler's bluff, for Beck and the others knew that Germany was by no means ready to wage a full-scale war. 'Peace in our time,' cried Chamberlain on his return to London, and the British people echoed his relief. But Goerdeler wrote at the time: 'If Britain and France had only taken upon themselves to risk war, Hitler would never have used force.' It was, he thought, 'absolute capitulation'.

That Hitler thought so too is evident from the events of the following year.

Having failed – or, as they felt, having been virtually betrayed by France and Britain to whom they considered they had given adequate warning of the situation – the small Resistance group adopted second line tactics during 1939. They attempted to fend off war in Europe. Less than two months after Munich, on 25th November, came the notorious, nationwide pogrom against the Jews. Hassell, lately retired from Rome and feeling his way with the opposition in Berlin, wrote in his private diary: 'I am most deeply troubled about the effect on our national life, which is dominated ever more inexorably

*Above left:* Hoepner, Panzer Commander and future victim of Hitler's retribution. *Above right:* Count von Helldorf, Police President of Berlin who was party to resistance plans. *Right above:* Mussolini, Hitler, his interpreter and Chamberlain at Munich, September 1938. *Right below:* Chamberlain flourishes the Munich agreement at Croydon airport

by a system capable of such things ... Respectable people were shocked to read names like Gürtner (Minister of Justice) and Schwerin-Krosigk (Minister of Finance) among the authors of the decree prescribing penalties for the Jews. These men cannot see apparently how they are degrading themselves and being used.'

He had found, for example, that Hjalmar Schacht, who (as we have seen) had just resigned from his dual position as President of the Reichsbank and Minister for Economic Affairs, was also bitterly opposed to Hitler. However, Schacht preferred to travel abroad and keep himself in the background.

By the turn of the year it was evident, except to those who were completely blind to affairs outside Germany, that France and Britain were rearming. Hitler meanwhile enhanced his prestige among the National Socialists and their camp followers by marching into Prague on 15th March 1939. Even Sir Nevile Henderson, the British Ambassador (who at this time was being treated for cancer of the mouth), felt bitter about Hitler's 'breach of faith'.

But Hitler was proceeding by intuition, not by the traditional rules of diplomatic negotiation, with their fine balances of international give and take. When he felt the walls of diplomacy to be crumbling, he seized what he wanted by lightning strokes which proved for a while to be more and more successful. Traditional diplomacy tended to give away completely before the *fait accompli*, which left no room for negotiation. His occupation of the demilitarized Rhineland in 1936, the Austrian Anschluss in 1938, the take-over of the Sudetenland in 1938, and now the occupation of Czechoslovakia in 1939 had all taken place without so much as a skirmish. The German people began to think Hitler was a magician with all the rabbits hidden in his hat. And so did Hitler himself, who from 1938 began to rely increasingly on his seemingly infallible intuition, unaided and unchecked by sound Intelligence reports from abroad. He began to discount any information which did not suit him, while his ministers and the more servile of the generals fed him only with what they thought he wanted to know. And what he wanted now, in the

Spring and Summer of 1939, was the capitulation of Poland.

Canaris, meanwhile, was concentrating his energies on the tactics necessary to prevent war breaking out in Europe as a result of Hitler's growing megalomania. He gained another important ally in the young lawyer, Fabian von Schlabrendorff, aged thirty-two in 1939, who had been opposed to Nazism since his student days, and whose views were solidly conservative and Christian. He was one of the few men who was not afraid of the regime, and had gone so far as to publish papers which opposed Hitler's policies. Most fortunately, he was one of the few active, front line men of the Resistance to survive, although at a terrible cost in suffering. His book, *Revolt against Hitler* (1948), published after the war and revised and published later as *The Secret War against Hitler* (1966) is one of the most reliable and informative first-hand accounts of the Resistance movement in Germany, more especially

*Above:* Sudeten Germans greet the Wehrmacht. *Right:* Hitler and his SS bodyguards among Sudetenlanders, 3rd October 1938

during the war years. His comment on the relationship of Canaris and Oster is revealing:
'Although Canaris hated Hitler and National Socialism, he himself did not feel capable of leading any decisive action against Hitler. Instead he protected Oster and allowed him to use the opportunities of the Counter-Intelligence, as far as it was under Oster's jurisdiction, to organize, strengthen, and enlarge the German resistance movement.'

Schlabrendorff was to be a stern critic of both the British and the French, whom he believes to have been completely spineless up to September 1939 as far as Hitler was concerned. He still believes that a stiffer attitude could have curbed his ambitions far more effectively during this key period than later, when the war itself had

Colonel Warlimont, Chief of the
Operations Section

started. Hitler himself became much
more isolated, more inaccessible to
reason, surrounded as he was by men
wholly committed to serving him,
such as Brauchitsch, Commander-in-
Chief of the Army, Wilhelm Keitel,
Alfred Jodl, and Walther Warlimont.
These men constituted the inner ring
of the High Command of the Armed
Forces (OKW). Only Halder and
another partially disaffected general,
Georg Thomas, kept more or less in
touch with Oster.

Spring and Summer of 1939 were a
period, therefore, in which little was
done but to issue warnings, conveyed
on a number of levels, to Britain and
the countries to the west of Germany
of the wrath to come in the East, particularly in Poland and Danzig. Among
these warnings was one which Ian
Colvin managed on 29th March to
put in person to the Prime Minister,
with help of the British Embassy
in Berlin and the Foreign Office.
Colvin received his hard information
of Hitler's intentions towards Poland
from Beck and Oster. This interview,
at least, appears to have achieved
its object; on 31st March it was
announced in the House of Commons that Britain and France would be
prepared to aid Poland if her in-
dependence were threatened. Hitler,
however, patently held this to be little
more than bluff, since bluff was what
he practised himself. He was open in
his loud-mouthed attacks on Poland,
while his plans to invade this recal-
citrant neighbour in the East became
more and more openly discussed with
his staff. At the same time he sought
between June and August to under-
cut any half-hearted attempts by
Britain and France to form an uneasy
alliance with Moscow by doing the
same thing himself. Stalin was as
cynical about such matters as Hitler,
and these men, the bitterest of rivals
for power in Europe, signed a non-
aggression treaty in August 1939 in
order to buy time for what was to be
the ultimate clash between them.

Meanwhile the messengers went
thick and fast from Berlin to London.
Goerdeler himself saw Churchill in
May and told him of the nature of the
German resistance. Later in the
summer Churchill also received
Schlabrendorff, who visited Britain
under cover of conducting research,
and also managed to see Lord Lloyd.
Churchill, who still held no office in
the Government, impressed Schlabrendorff with his vigour:

'Churchill's appearance, his way of
conducting the conversation his rapid-
fire questions and answers, all made a
deep impression on me. I had the feeling that I was in the presence of a
statesman of historic stature. Unlike
Lord Lloyd, Churchill avoided all
personalities; and he also displayed
none of Lloyd's doubts about the
strength and determination of his
country. On the contrary, Churchill
seemed confident that the English
nation was basically sound and fully
capable of putting up a good fight . . .
'During the course of our conversation, he displayed great interest in
the German opposition. Finally he
asked whether I could guarantee a
successful action by our group. The
answer to that question was not easy
for me, and I hesitated for a moment

Ian Colvin, the British journalist whom the resistance approached

Fabian von Schlabrendorff, another aristocratic German

before replying in the negative, but I felt that it was most important to remain realistic and not give in to wishful thinking. In view of the difficulties of living under a tyranny, and at the same time working towards its overthrow, it seemed impossible to guarantee a successful *coup d'état*. I believe, by the way, that Churchill fully realized these problems, and that his question was meant to test my reaction.'

Others who went to Britain at this time included Adam von Trott zu Solz, a scholar who had studied at Oxford, and the Count Helmuth von Moltke, who was half-British and had for a while been a member of the English bar. Both of these men loved Britain and were among the German intellectuals who despised Hitler and detested what he was doing to their country. Moltke was to create his own centre of opposition in the form of the circle of intellectuals who met normally at Kreisau, his country estate. They were for the most part dedicated to non-violence.

This was the position as Europe drifted into a state of war. 'Prague', said Henderson to Hassell in private, 'was the straw that broke the camel's back. Now it is impossible for Chamberlain to fly here again with his umbrella.' The German non-aggression pact with Russia, signed on 22nd August, conceded a second, secret agreement in which various spheres of interest in the East were defined, including the division of Poland between Germany and the Soviet Union. Nothing could stop Hitler now that Russia's teeth were, for the moment, drawn. Attempts by Beck and others to intervene with the High Command were merely repulsed. Hitler's armies entered Poland at 04.45 hours on the morning of 1st September, and within three weeks all was over with this proud and independently-minded country.

To Hitler's annoyance, however, Britain and France declared war on Germany. Canaris just managed to warn the British military attaché in Berlin that an air-raid on London was planned for 3rd September before the Embassy staff broke up. But Halder managed to get the air-raid cancelled, and the uneasy period of the 'phoney' war began, during which Oster, with Canaris's knowledge, was to do everything he could at great personal risk to pre-warn the countries to the West of Germany of what was in store for them. Canaris, in particular, had now to play a double game – controlling the real activities of the Abwehr while at the same time using it to frustrate as far as possible Hitler's intentions in the West, as he saw them developing. He was horrified by what was taking place in Poland. Goerdeler told Hassell that Canaris, 'came back from Poland entirely broken'. The natural melancholy of his nature was intensified, and he was to endure bouts of deep depression.

In August, when the war was imminent, he had hastened to recruit Dohnanyi to the Central Office, Department Z of the Abwehr, and Dohnanyi (given the rank of a major) and Oster (now a major-general) were to become close associates in the planning of future resistance activity. Dohnanyi was quiet, reserved, and exact; he was a liberal Christian, but opposed to any kind of radicalism. The heads of several of the Abwehr departments were of like mind with

Canaris – for example, Colonel Hans Pieckenbrock, head of external espionage, Colonel Georg Hanson, his successor, Colonel Hans Grosscurth, head of sabotage abroad, Colonel Erwin Lahousen, and others. But even these resistance loyalists had to carry out their normal duties as cover for the rest – for example, it was Pieckenbrock who conducted negotiations concerning the invasion of Norway with Quisling in Copenhagen.

Although the idea of a *coup* staged by a resolute group of generals in the High Command was for a while revived by Beck, Canaris and Oster, their chief link at OKW, General Halder, proved in the end inadequate. Hitler's hold on his generals was by now all but complete, and they grew increasingly afraid of him with his sudden demands and outbursts of rage, and his threats of dismissal. They were wedded to their careers, their rank, their pay, their pensions and privileges. Plans for the *coup d'état* were actually sketched out afresh by

*eft:* **Helmuth von Moltke.**
*bove:* **Molotov signs the ten-year
non-aggression pact with Germany,
August 1939**

Oster (the Oster study, as it came to
be called), and a small network of
officers in a position to deploy men
was gradually built up.

Parallel with these plans, which
were to be frustrated because no
general in high place could be in-
duced to give a lead, were various
attempts to institute peace negotiations with Britain. Hassell, working on
his own, made a personal attempt
through an acquaintance of Lord
Halifax, a man called J Lonsdale
Bryans whom he met, with Halifax's
knowledge and rather grudging consent, in Switzerland in February 1940,
and later in April, after the German
invasion of Denmark and Norway
rendered any such discussions
abortive.

More significant than Hassell's lone
speculation in peace were the prolonged attempts by one of Canaris's
most trusted agents, Dr Josef Müller,
a Munich lawyer, and a staunch
Catholic, to win the consent of Pope
Pius XII to act as an intermediary in
possible peace negotiations. Müller,
who went to Rome in October 1939,
acted principally through Father
Robert Leiber, a German Jesuit at the
Vatican, though Müller was in fact
known personally to the Pope, who
was familiar with Germany since he
had been Papal Nuncio in Berlin during
the 1920s, and was acquainted with
both Beck and Canaris. They had met
while exercising their horses, the
future Pope having been a keen rider
during his term of duty in Germany.
The Pope was, if anything, a Germano-
phile as well as a trained diplomat,
having prior to his elevation acted as
Cardinal Secretary of State from
1930-39. Müller met with little resis-

tance in the Vatican; his negotiations came to be known to the inner corps of the Resistance by the code name of Operation X.

In spite of his prejudices in favour of Germany, the Pope was by now deeply disturbed by the behaviour of Hitler's forces in Poland. The British Minister at the Vatican, Sir Francis D'Arcy Osborne, was informed of these unofficial peace overtures from Germany, and reported on them to Britain. Like Hassell, Müller was concerned to outline the basic conditions on which peace with Britain might be established, and these proposed conditions received the tacit approval of the Pope. These terms as set down were called the X Memorandum; copies were prepared in Rome for both Berlin and London, and a version of this was finally put before Brauchitsch by

Halder. 'This is pure treason,' exclaimed Brauchitsch, and refused to consider the document further. The German copy was preserved by an officer greatly trusted by the Resistance, Colonel Werner Schrader. But these attempts to arrive at peace negotiations, like those by Hassell, were rendered abortive when Hitler invaded Scandinavia.

Oster meantime had been doing what he could to save the situation. Using his friend, Colonel Jacobus Sas, the Dutch military attaché in Berlin, as his intermediary, he passed on a series of warnings to Denmark, Norway and the Netherlands, giving the actual dates planned for their invasion, dates which, owing to Hitler's constant postponements of action, were not initially proved correct. Warnings were also issued via the Vatican by Müller, who received his information from Oster. Strangely enough, the German monitoring service intercepted the Belgian envoy's coded message, and both the SD and

*Above:* German assault pioneers tackle a wire entanglement. *Below:* German reconnaissance troops in France, May 1940. *Right:* Hitler on his victory tour of Paris, July 1940. He never revisited the city

**General Henning von Tresckow**

(ironically) the Abwehr were informed that a German agent at the Vatican was passing on top secret information. Canaris, with a stroke of genius, placed the investigation of the leakage in the hands of Müller! This, however, was not the end of the story: another somewhat officious Abwehr agent handed in a report which placed the blame for the leakage squarely on Müller's shoulders, and Canaris had arbitrarily to suppress his evidence. Finally, on 3rd May Oster gave Sas the final date for the invasion of Holland; this Sas passed on in code to the Dutch War Office in The Hague. The invasion came, as finally predicted, on 10th May.

A period of stalemate set in for the conspirators. The fall in June of France, Belgium and the Netherlands, following so hard upon that of Denmark and Norway in April, made Hitler seem impregnable. In July Rumania, with her valuable oil-fields, placed herself under German protection, following a partial invasion by Russia. Hedged in by his generals, and secured by his own increasingly secluded way of life, it seemed impossible any longer to think of Hitler as vulnerable. Between June 1940 and June 1941, the month of the offensive

against Russia (for whose fate Canaris and his associates cared rather less) the plans of the conspirators turned increasingly in the direction of out-and-out assassination of the Führer by a single agent, or a small, determined group. The previous plan for a military *coup d'état* followed by Hitler's trail in a public court, was by now obviously impossible. A great part of Germany would have rallied to his defence and freed him. The older wing of the Resistance gradually came to agree with the younger – Hitler must be assassinated. A small minority, including Goerdeler, were never to believe it right to kill him; it went against the grain of their traditional Christian belief. But the civilians in any case could attempt nothing; only those in the Army who came into some form of contact with Hitler, were in any position to take violent action against him.

When during the summer of 1940 the invasion of Britain was postponed indefinitely, Hitler turned his full attention to preparations for his massive campaign against the Soviet Union. On the Eastern front, the conspirators' hopes began to centre round another young staff officer, Major-General Henning von Tresckow, to whom Schlabrendorff, now in the Army, had been appointed ADC. Tresckow was aged only forty; he was a man of great sensitivity and profoundly opposed to Hitler. As a staff officer, he was in close touch with Field Marshal von Kluge, now, at the advanced age of sixty, Commander of one of the seven Army Corps charged with the responsibility of conducting the forthcoming blitzkrieg on Russia. Only two years before, at the time of the Blomberg-Fritsch crisis, Kluge had been one of the generals Hitler had dismissed as hostile to his plans, though he did not, of course, know that he wavered on the borderland of the Resistance. Now he had been restored, and given the rank of Field Marshal as a sop to his pride. As Hitler had vacillated over him, so he was now

*Above:* Waffen SS soldiers dead in the Russian snow, December 1941. *Below:* A German anti-partisan patrol in Russia

Field-Marshal von Kluge,
Commander of the German Second
Army

Pastor Bonhoeffer, the great theologian
who was to be executed for resistance
activity

to vacillate over Hitler, weighing his own security and self-interest in the scales of expediency. Nevertheless, he was the highest-ranking Commander on the Eastern front to be in direct contact with members of the Resistance, and Tresckow acted as the goad to his conscience, while Schlabrendorff kept in touch with the men in Berlin.

This was the position during the fearful winter of 1941-42, when Kluge's Army Group, which was in the thick of the advance on Moscow, was frozen into immobility only twenty-two miles from their objective. Kluge, in spite of Hitler's orders to the contrary, was forced to order a partial withdrawal; Hitler himself had taken over executive command of the Army when Brauchitsch suffered a heart attack. Meanwhile Germany's fate was being sealed; Hitler seemed barely to notice it when the United States declared war on him in December, after the Japanese attack on Pearl Harbor. Canaris concentrated successfully on keeping Franco's Spain out of the war; he was to be in Spain frequently between 1940 and 1943, ostensibly acting as Hitler's special representative to negotiate Spain's involvement as Hitler's ally. But Canaris was an expert in hedging, and knew how to persuade others to hedge also. In addition, he kept up his acquaintance with Heydrich's successor, Walther Schellenberg, after Heydrich's assassination in Prague in May 1942; he managed to maintain his good name with the SS and SD to the last possible moment. He knew, too, how to keep away from Berlin, where Oster was always ready to take charge. He was ceaselessly on the move, usually in the Mediterranean area, warming his small body in the sun. He always wore an overcoat in the height of summer. One of his assistants described him at this time as, 'very bright, animated and talkative, like a little old lady'. But he managed to keep his nerve in spite of the most dangerous double game he and his associates were playing. Oster had sent a secret warning to Belgrade in April 1941 in anticipation of Hitler's lightning attack on Yugoslavia and Greece just prior to the invasion of Russia. Like Canaris, Goerdeler was constantly on the move, but he was far less discreet

*Above:* Heydrich's cortege passing through Berlin, June 1942. *Below:* Heydrich's State Funeral. His assassination led to terrible reprisals

in voicing his views, proselytising everyone he knew, writing endless memoranda and letters, and drawing up shadow governments to take over on Hitler's downfall.

The Resistance leaders were naturally highly responsive to the ebb and flow of events, in so far as they could assess them from their centre in Berlin, supplemented by the relatively wider, more international viewpoint of Canaris and Goerdeler. Although Hitler's Germany seemed at the height of its powers – its empire now stretching from the Atlantic seaboard of France to deep into Russia and the Caucasus, and from the northern fiords of Norway to the occupied territories of the Mediterranean and North Africa – those with knowledge were well aware that Hitler was now beginning to extend his military resources beyond their capacity to be effectively aggressive. The attempts by the Resistance to make terms with Britain were frustrated partly by Churchill's determination that Germany should surrender unconditionally (which was very difficult from the kind of terms originally envisaged by Müller or Hassell), and partly by the Allied agreement of January 1942, that no one of them would sign a separate peace with Germany. Nevertheless in May 1942, Pastor Bonhoeffer of the Abwehr, representing the Resistance, met Bishop Bell of Britain in neutral Sweden and gave him details of the Resistance inside Germany, pleading in vain for signs of official, public recognition by Churchill or the British government once Bell had passed on the information he had been given.

On the other hand, the tide began to turn against Hitler between May 1942, the month when the thousand-bomber raids by the RAF first took their toll on German cities and industry, and the end of January 1943, when, contrary to Hitler's explicit orders,

**General von Paulus, Commander of the Sixth Army, who surrendered Stalingrad**

Field-Marshal Paulus surrendered in Stalingrad. Rommel had also met his first serious reverse at El Alamein in North Africa. The Resistance, too, had its first major reverse: Wilhelm Schmidthuber, Müller's associate in the negotiations at the Vatican, was foolish enough to commit certain serious currency offences. His arrest and interrogation led to the discovery by the Gestapo that Müller, and worse still Dohnanyi, had been involved in matters which might be regarded as treasonable. Investigations proceeded slowly and agonisingly throughout the winter of 1942-43, and, with Canaris nervous as a cat and Oster expressing his anxiety through excessive bravado, the Resistance felt the time was now more than ripe for hard action. The trial and execution of Hans and Sophie Scholl and their university associates in February 1943 were to add to the conspirator's determination to act, though the Scholls had had no direct link with the 'official' Resistance. Hitler must be killed. But how?

They turned to Tresckow and Schlabrendorff as their surest, most immediate hope, and the pattern for the *coup d'état* was settled in a form which was to prevail during the key period of the activities of the Resistance during the years 1943 and 1944 Tresckow and Schlabrendorff would take responsibility (if possible with the backing of Kluge) for the assassination when Hitler was on one of his rare visits to the Eastern front. Schlabrendorff continued to act as liaison between Berlin and the Eastern front and, when necessary, with Resistance associates at Hitler's headquarters at Rastenburg in East Prussia. In Berlin, a new and most important ally based on the War Office was General Olbricht, Chief of Supplies for the Reserve Army commanded by General Fromm, who was, unfortunately, wholly unreliable from the point of view of the Resistance. However, with men of the calibre of Beck, Hassell, Schacht and Goerdeler

Fromm, who tried unsuccessfully to cover his tracks on 20th July

Olbricht, the Reserve Army General in league with the conspirators

as the initial heads of a caretaker government, it was assumed the generals on all fronts would willingly give their support once Hitler was safely out of the way. Beyond this, the Resistance planned very little in 1943.

Tresckow (whom Schlabrendorff used to call the watchmaker because he had to wind up Kluge's flagging opposition to Hitler every day) met Canaris and Dohnanyi early in 1943 at Smolensk, where Kluge's Centre Army Group was based; Canaris covered this meeting by organizing a conference of Intelligence Officers. It was agreed a group of officers led by Baron Georg von Boeselager should surround and assassinate Hitler when he visited the Eastern front on 13th March. All was set for this attempt when Kluge at the last minute, though still sympathetic to Hitler's removal by other means, refused his own direct collaboration.

It was then decided that Tresckow and Schlabrendorff should act on their own initiative, smuggling a bomb onto the aircraft in which Hitler would fly back to Rastenburg. The Abwehr pro-

vided the necessary time-bomb – a plastic bomb captured from British supplies and activated by a time-fuse controlled by acid which disintegrated a length of wire. The thickness of the wire determined the time between initial contact of the acid and the metal of the wire and the release of the striking-pin held by the wire onto the detonator. Three thicknesses of wire were provided to ensure delays of ten minutes, half an hour and two hours between activation and detonation. A number of these bombs were brought on the occasion of the Intelligence Officers' Conference at Smolensk. Since neither Tresckow nor Schlabrendorff were trained to handle such weapons, certain secret tests had to be devised. The test bombs proved remarkably effective, though the fuse-timing did not prove reliable in the intense cold of the Russian winter. However, the particular virtue of these bombs was that their time-fuse operated in complete silence.

Two of these bombs, which had something like the square shape of a Cointreau bottle, were parcelled up together and stored in Schlabrendorff's quarters. Hitler arrived by plane on the morning of 13th March, flying with his doctor and certain members of his staff from Rastenburg. The flight took about two hours. He held his conference with Kluge before lunch. During lunch Schlabrendorff asked a junior staff officer travelling with Hitler if he would take two bottles of Cointreau back as a present for General Helmuth Stieff, an administrative officer at Rastenburg. Schlabrendorff then signalled the word, 'Flash' to Dohnanyi in Berlin, and went to pick up the parcel of bombs to take to the runway. Tresckow was there to watch Schlabrendorff hand over the parcel to Hitler's aide, having first activated the fuse attached to one of the bombs. Hitler was airborne, with the bombs aboard the aircraft; he had an escort of fighters. Schlabrendorff hastened to telephone his colleagues in Berlin to stand by.

The catastrophe was due to take place somewhere over Minsk. The conspirators expected the fighter escort to signal the destruction of Hitler's aircraft. But the minutes went by. Schlabrendorff and Tresckow waited in Smolensk; Beck, Oster and the rest in Berlin. An hour passed. Then a further half hour. Then two hours. There was still neither message nor signal.

After two hours, Tresckow found an excuse to telephone Rastenburg. He learned that Hitler had arrived quite safely; nothing untoward had happened. It was an appalling disappointment. What had gone wrong with the bombs? The package was now presumably in Stieff's hands. Had he opened it? Tresckow got through to the officer carrying the parcel. He had not, as it happened, had time yet to hand it over. Tresckow told him at once a mistake had been made in Smolensk – the wrong package had been given him. Would he please keep the package in his possession till someone from Smolensk could retrieve it? Certainly, he said.

The following day Schlabrendorff flew to Rastenburg. Never were two real bottles of Cointreau so willingly handed over. The package of bombs retrieved, Schlabrendorff travelled that night by sleeper to Berlin. In the sleeping compartment he hastened to undo the parcel to see what had gone wrong. He removed the time-fuse and examined it. There was a small fault in the mechanism; the detonator had not worked when the firing-pin had struck it.

On 15th March Schlabrendorff met Oster and Dohnanyi in Berlin and showed them the fuse the failure of which was to cost so many millions of men, women and children their lives. The holocaust of genocide in the concentration camps was to continue at full strength, while the fighting front in the East was to cost countless Russian and German lives. In Germany, tens of thousands were to die through the mounting fury of the air raids.

Such opportunities as this to kill Hitler were few and far between. But the same month Baron Rudolf von Gersdorff volunteered for a suicide mission. He was prepared to blow himself up along with Hitler while the Führer was attending an exhibition of captured Russian war materials in Berlin. He failed to get anywhere near Hitler, whose visit was brief and perfunctory. Olbrich complained, meanwhile, that even if these attempts had succeeded, the organisation for the take-over of the administration in Berlin was still inadequate. Tresckow travelled to Berlin, ostensibly on sick leave, to review the details of this aspect of the plan. He was soon to have a young officer draughted to help him – Colonel Count Claus von Stauffenberg.

The second generation in the Resistance was beginning to take over from the first.

*Above:* Hitler, Mussolini and Ribbentrop lunch together at a Russian aerodrome.
*Below:* Hitler and Mussolini review the Italian Expeditionary force, Russia July 1941
*Right:* Hitler, the triumphant

# The Gestapo and the defence of Hitler

**The SS Leibstandarte changing guard in the courtyard of the new Reich Chancellery**

Men who seek to assassinate the head of a police state have to resolve many problems. Some of these have already emerged in the particular case of the conspiracy to kill Hitler – the oath of personal loyalty which made even those most critical of his regime hesitate to take any direct action against him, the almost total lack of access to his person open to key members of the conspiracy, the way in which he was always surrounded by a small circle of men and women who were utterly devoted to him. But additional to these factors was the very special nature of the man himself.

Hitler was not only dictator of a great part of Europe, he was also in many respects an eccentric recluse who created his own extraordinary and rigidly enclosed pattern of living. He was by nature a petit bourgeois retaining many of his suburban habits within the grandeur of the great dwellings which went with his exalted position – the Chancellery in Berlin and his elaborate and luxurious mountain retreat in Berchtesgaden. With little warning to his staff, he moved from the one place to the other, varying this only by periods of residence at his Army headquarters, of which the chief at this time was Rastenburg in East Prussia, some 300 miles by air from Berlin. Wherever he was (and he spent weeks and even months on end at Berchtesgaden) he often turned night into day – staying up to talk endlessly into the small hours of the night to the intimate circle of nonentities who hung on his words, which included his pathetic and colourless little mistress, Eva Braun, and then sleeping on until late into the morning, or resting for prolonged periods in the afternoon, after a comparatively late lunch. He became increasingly self-centred, relying less and less on expert advice likely to contradict his own set views, in fact distrusting all experts and relying on his notorious intuitive judgment unsupported by really accurate intelligence from the war fronts. As the war

began to turn against him in 1943 he resented bad news, and much he should have known and taken into account was in consequence withheld from him by Keitel and others who feared to become the hated bearers of ill tidings.

He had therefore to be assassinated by the conspirators either in the Chancellery or at Bechtesgaden or in one of his various headquarters, or while in transit between these places. Since all his journeys were undertaken suddenly and quite unpredictably, so that even the police were seldom notified of the route he would take, to catch him while on the move would be exceptionally difficult. His visits to the battlefronts were equally unpredictable, and increasingly rare. He was, of course, well aware that attempts upon his life might be made, and he naturally determined to offer an assassin the least possible opportunity to penetrate his defences. No dates were normally announced for his sudden arrivals and departures.

He was also closely guarded by picked men of the SS, including his personal bodyguards when he was on the move or in any kind of more general company. No visitor could come into his presence armed. To draw a concealed gun, take aim and shoot him was virtually impossible, though there were several brave men who volunteered to undertake this, if necessary, suicide mission.

The Gestapo was permanently on the watch, therefore, for isolated would-be assassins – whether madmen, fanatics, Communists, or other political opponents – rather than for any widespread conspiracy to wrest power out of his hands. They had to be prepared for any eventuality, including the kind of commando mission introduced from outside Germany which had led to the assassination of Heydrich while driving through the streets of Prague in an open staff-car. When an abortive attempt by an unknown, lone marksman was made on Goebbels' life in 1943, Hitler gave his

Minister of Propaganda and Public Enlightenment a stern warning about letting himself become a target, and then made him a Christmas present of a heavily armoured car.

It may be wondered why so much could be said, if not done, with impunity by so many individuals, some of whom, like Goerdeler, Stauffenberg, and even Oster himself, were not prone to keep their views wholly to themselves and their circle of mutual friends. The brighter men in the Gestapo were well aware that a state of conspiracy against the regime was a possible factor with which they must at some stage contend. They had therefore to keep continuous watch upon suspects of every kind, high and low alike. But this did not mean that those under suspicion would be arrested the moment the first shreds of evidence against them came into the hands of the Gestapo. Far from it; provided the conspirators were only just conspiring, and not poised for immediate action, the Gestapo considered them for the most part far more valuable left at large than put in places of confinement. They might even be encouraged just a little, in order that their activities could be watched and their contacts noted. The Gestapo, of course, was notorious for making sudden swoops in the small hours of the night. They were also notorious for playing cat-and-mouse with their more valuable suspects.

Nor was this all. Wheels were geared to circle within wheels. At one stage the civilian wing of the Resistance seriously considered attempting to bring Himmler into the conspiracy, in which case the cat and the mouse would hunt together. The conspirators realised that the men at the top – especially Goebbels, Göring, and Himmler – each regarded himself as the true successor to Hitler should the latter's health or reason fail, should he die suddenly or be assassinated. Though Göring was Hitler's legal heir, he was in disfavour with everyone because of his failure as leader of the Luftwaffe to protect Germany in the air raids and because of his propensity for drugs. There was no doubt that Himmler, by far the most fanatically dedicated of the three to essential Nazi principles, was also the best placed to seize power for himself. He had all the police, secret and otherwise, at his command, and the SS contingents serving within the armed forces, the Waffen-SS, were also technically his men.

As for Goebbels, he had no forces at his disposal, and only the respect due to his vituperative tongue and dangerous intelligence might gain him any position with the others should Hitler disappear. As the civilian conspirators studied their enemies for a useful, if temporary ally, they came to the conclusion that Himmler might be worth approaching, however gingerly this was done. Many SS officers were known to be cynical about the war now that the tables were turning against Germany. So on 26th August 1943, Dr Johannes Popitz, Finance Minister for Prussia and one of the less prominent but still useful men among the civilians hostile to Hitler, found himself being introduced to Himmler. The man who had brought this about was Carl Langbehn, a member of the fringe of the Resistance who, in another capacity, had undertaken some intelligence work for Himmler.

Various and contradictory accounts survive of what took place at this strange meeting, but it would seem that Popitz in effect urged Himmler, as the most 'responsible' man in the Nazi hierarchy, to rescue Germany from continuing this self-destructive war. In spite of Hitler's undoubted 'genius', said Popitz tactfully, the war could not be continued successfully because corruption on all sides was undermining the Führer's plans – farseeing, of course, as these naturally were. Popitz appears to have advanced these tentative arguments before an intent, prim, but virtually silent Himmler – who was well aware in any case that Poptiz was one of the Gestapo's suspects. The upshot was that Himmler was requested to consider, in Hitler's own interests as well as the German nation's, undertaking some form of peace negotiations behind the Führer's back. It was true that Himmler had indeed, very evasively, been considering some such action on his own private account, and Langbehn had known of this; but Himmler in such dangerous matters always retreated farther than he advanced, held back by an agony of indecision. He was, in fact, worried to death about the state of Hitler's health and (dare he admit it?) his reason.

Perhaps it was the long years of frustration which led to this abortive contact with Himmler, an act bordering on desperation which Langbehn and Popitz were later arrested and ultimately hanged for their pains, while Himmler retired increasingly into the cloud cuckoo land of playing at peace negotiations with the Allies without actually committing himself to any serious discussions.

What Himmler was determined to do, however, was destroy the Abwehr, and take over for himself the handling of all Intelligence. It was important, therefore, to tighten the net around the men directly associated with the Abwehr, whose loyalty to the regime was at all suspect.

As early as April 1942 Hassell, too, had been officially warned by Ernst von Weiszäcker, Senior State Secretary in the Foreign Ministry, that he was being watched by the Gestapo. The atmosphere of fear is conveyed by the agitated manner in which this very senior civil servant conveyed the warning, as Hassell described it in his diary:

'He carefully closed the windows and doors, and announced with some emphasis that he had a very serious

The Berghof, Hitler's villa at Berchtesgarten

The Reich Chancellery, designed by
Albert Speer, floodlit at night

**Early holiday snaps of Eva Braun, Hitler's mistress and eventual wife**

Hassell was not easily frightened, but he laid low at once, and even discontinued writing his diary for a while. Another suspect was Goerdeler, whom the Gestapo by now were watching closely. His indiscretions were so well known that Goerdeler, far more even than Hassell, was too hot to know.

During the period 1942-43 the Gestapo began to close in. Their first major success was not against the Abwehr itself, but against the largely Communist spy ring which came to be known as the Rote Kapelle, or Red Band organisation. As soon as war had broken out between Germany and the Soviet Union, the objective of Communist agents in the Reich was not to assassinate Hitler or to stage a *coup* in their own right, but to assist in the ultimate victory of the Russian armies. The various Rote Kapelle 'cells' supplied intelligence likely to be of use to Russia, and used short-wave transmitters to pass it on to the Soviet Union. Canaris, in fact, used the Abwehr to assist Himmler's Gestapo to ferret out the German agents of the Rote Kapelle, who were finally arrested in August 1942. One of them turned out to be a colourful, bohemian character called Harro Schulze-Boysen, who held a staff appointment in Göring's Luftwaffe. The interrogator appointed to investigate the more prominent of these Communist agents was Dr Manfred Roeder, an exceptionally keen-minded and ruthless investigator, and the same who was later to probe into the affairs of Schmidhuber, Dohnanyi and the Abwehr.

The second exposure was a far easier one – the tragic case of Hans and Sophie Scholl already referred to. They represented the dedicated opponents to Nazism among the more idealistic youth of Germany. In 1942, the year of their arrest and execution, Hans was twenty-five and his sister only twenty-two, and they spread their anti-Hitler propaganda among the students at Munich University.

matter to discuss with me. He brusquely waved aside my joking rejoinder. For the time being he had to ask me to spare him the embarrassment of my presence. When I started to remonstrate he interrupted me harshly . . . Every time I asked for enlightenment he cut me short . . . He then proceeded to heap reproaches on me as he paced excitedly up and down. I had been unbelievably indiscreet, quite unheard-of; as a matter of fact, "with all due deference", so had my wife. This was all known in certain places (the Gestapo), and they claimed even to have documents. He must demand, most emphatically, that I correct this behaviour . . . He paid no attention to my objection that he seemed to associate himself with these unsubstantiated accusations . . . I had no idea, he said, how people were after me (the Gestapo). Every step I took was observed. I should certainly burn everything I had in the way of notes which covered conversations in which one or other had said this or that. Apparently he meant himself. He opposed my efforts to get at the facts behind all this; this concerned my future behaviour, not the past. Finally he said: "Now, *auf Wiedersehen*, but please not too soon!"' '

The Gestapo had watched them for a period, and knew their close associates. On 22nd February 1943 they were tried by the notorious Nazi judge Roland Freisler, in Hitler's so-called People's Court. Freisler's trials were little more than violent recriminations which he hoped would reduce his victims to a state of guilty collapse. He shouted at those brought before him; his hearings were nothing but acts of intimidation. The Scholls readily admitted their guilt in order to spare as far as possible those associated with them, but a hundred arrests followed their own, and there were to be further executions. Their movement, known as the White Rose, revealed a widespread opposition to Hitler in university and intellectual circles, and the Scholls became, like so many individuals who acted spontaneously against the regime, in effect political martyrs. Hassell, in particular, was deeply moved by their death, especially as he was now trying his best to link up the older generation, such as he, Canaris and Beck represented, with the younger generation among the believers in resistance, especially Moltke, Trott, and Count Peter Yorck, who had married a school-friend of the Bonhoeffers and Dohnanyi. Yorck, in fact, was sent on a secret mission to neutral Switzerland in January 1943 to meet Allen Dulles, Roosevelt's representative, and urge that the Allies be more forthcoming and helpful in their response to the efforts of the Resistance. But his mission, like that of Bonhoeffer in Sweden the previous year, proved abortive.

The older generation were beginning to suffer from more than nervous strain. Beck, the man whom all regarded as the leader of the Resistance movement, was operated upon for cancer of the stomach in March 1943. According to Hassell, Beck was so deeply suspect by the Gestapo that a secret watch was kept on him even while he was in hospital. The Gestapo indeed, questioned the distinguished surgeon who operated upon him, Professor Ferdinand Sauerbruch, who was one of Beck's friends. Canaris, too, had to be extremely cautious. Himmler had told him he had believed for some while that a group of influential officers was planning a *coup;* he added that he had thought it wise to wait a while and see how things developed. He believed that Beck and Goerdeler were at the back of it, but there was still time (he had said) to hold back so that the whole ring might be discovered.

Canaris was not only deeply disturbed by this news, but also by the prolonged investigations into this most unfortunate case of Schmidhuber's currency offences. This, as we have seen, was now being probed by the keen mind of Roeder, fresh from his success with the Rote Kapelle. He too seemed quite prepared to take his time; Schmidhuber also seemed ready to talk. He was to prove a very weak link in the Abwehr chain. Even Oster began to worry. In February 1943 Canaris himself had to face questioning by Ernst Kaltenbrunner, Himmler's newly-appointed head of Reich Security, about the political reliability of certain of his staff. He was able to hedge by claiming that it was his agents' duty to mix with dubious company. How else could intelligence be gleaned?

So the winter months of 1942-43 passed in an atmosphere of tension and anxiety, heightened by the failure of Beck's health, the trial and executions of the Scholls, and finally in March (the month of Beck's operation for cancer), the failure of Tresckow's and Schlabrendorff's attempt on Hitler's life. This the Gestapo knew nothing about – nor of Baron Gersdorff's suicide mission, which, as we have seen, failed through lack of opportunity to approach Hitler's person. Then suddenly, on 5th April, Roeder's investigations bore their evil fruit, and the Gestapo decided to strike.

Roeder, whose suspicions of a small-

**Himmler, head of the SS, inspects prisoners of war on the Russian front**

scale conspiracy rooted in the Abwehr probably had not matured before March, realized that Schmidhuber was a petty cog in a somewhat larger machine. The Gestapo, as stated previously, had a bias in their minds that potential insurrection was likely to originate with individuals rather than organized groups. But Schmidhuber, terrified by months of incarceration in the Tegel military prison in Berlin and by the continual pressure of interrogations probing into his small crimes, gradually began to reveal something (but not all) of the activities in which Müller, Bonhoeffer and Dohnanyi had been involved. An investigation which was initially concerned solely with the currency offences gradually turned into a political enquiry. Warnings from many sources, spoken in whispers, reached the ears of Canaris, Oster and Dohnanyi alike.

Beck, who was a meticulous man, insisted that the Resistance keep itself fully documented in order, when the time came, to prove the length to which discussions had gone to remove Hitler and restore peace, as well as the seriousness with which the task of forming a caretaker government had been approached. The files also had to include incontrovertible evidence against the worst Nazi offenders, so that they might be exposed as speedily as possible and brought to trial. Only papers connected with current discussions were normally kept in the safe in Dohnanyi's office at Abwehr headquarters in Berlin. The rest were gradually accumulated in a special safe at the High Command's headquarters in Zossen, near Berlin. When Dohnanyi began to realize, early in 1942, that he was being watched, he avoided going to Zossen. Oster, like Canaris, was not in favour of keeping too many incriminating documents at any place where there was the remotest danger of them being found;

he went to Zossen as if on normal business and purged the safe of everything which could be spared. Nevertheless, it seemed that only too much had to be kept.

On 5th April Roeder, accompanied by a Gestapo officer, Franz Xaver Sonderegger, called without warning at the Abwehr offices. They asked to see Canaris, who (as Roeder was to put it later) received them in a very gentlemanly fashion. Producing a search warrant, Roeder asked Canaris to take him immediately to Dohnanyi's office.

What followed has been the subject of many varying accounts. When Heinrich Fraenkel was investigating this subject for our book, *The Canaris Conspiracy*, he checked all the various versions carefully with Roeder himself, and we are satisfied that our published account is accurate. The details given here appear to be the truth of the matter. Dohnanyi's room could only be reached by passing through Oster's office. Canaris, therefore, led Roeder and Sonderegger first of all to Oster, who accompanied the others into Dohnanyi's presence. Dohnanyi rose to his feet at this unannounced, unexpected intrusion. While Sonderegger stood guard, and Canaris and Oster could only act as silent and serious-faced witnesses, Roeder stepped forward, stated he had a warrant to search the office, and asked Dohnanyi to open the drawers of his desk and the door of his safe. Dohnanyi hesitated, and either out of nervousness or perhaps deliberately to give himself time to think, appeared to have to search for his keys, which he finally produced from his trouser pocket. Then Roeder began the task of looking through the papers in the desk and safe. Sonderegger saw Dohnanyi try to signal Oster with his eyes to indicate a particular paper lying on the desk, Rather clumsily, to say the least, Oster endeavoured to take possession of this document while Roeder was looking at some files. Sonderegger gave a warning,

and Oster had to relinquish the paper; it had written on it one of the many outline-plans for the administration of Germany after Hitler's removal. It was marked with the letter 'O' in coloured pencil. Roeder, seeing some coloured pencils on Oster's desk, confiscated these before he left after a search which lasted two hours. There was sufficient Resistance documentation in Dohnanyi's office to warrant his immediate arrest. He was taken to the Tegel military jail.

Roeder overlooked only one important clue in Dohnanyi's office – the key to his secret safe in Zossen. This was kept tied in a folder which appeared only to be concerned with matters of routine. Oster salvaged it the moment Roeder and Sonderegger had gone. However, the papers Roeder had taken away contained evidence which led to the arrest of Dohnanyi's wife, Christine, her brother, Dietrich Bonhoeffer, and Josef Müller and his wife. Oster was not arrested, but suspended from duty and placed under grave suspicion. It was dangerous now to associate with him, and he was expressly forbidden to go to the Abwehr or make contact with its officers. The two women, however, were eventually released when their interrogations were completed with no results useful to the case.

The intensive interrogations which followed built up into a case which Roeder called the Schwarz Kapelle, or Black Band, investigation. They were conducted principally by himself and Sonderegger during the period April to August 1943. Otto John, a most knowledgeable member of the conspiracy, volunteered after the war the statement given below which makes it clear that the important thing for the prisoners was to keep themselves detained by the military, and avoid at all costs being handed over to the Gestapo. Nevertheless, Roeder (who actually represented the Luftwaffe Judiciary, but was retained for this strictly Army case because of his experience with the Rote Kapelle)

The flak waggon of the Führer's personal train in which he normally travelled about the Reich

Above: Johannes Popitz, ex-Prussian Finance Minister on trial 1944. *Below left:* Weizsäcker, German diplomat and resistance worker. *Below right:* Roland Freisler, President of the People's Court which condemned the Scholls

proved a harsher investigator than Sonderegger of the Gestapo. A great deal of information about their methods was revealed in official enquiries set up after the war into their activities. Evidence was given by those members of the group in the Resistance who most fortunately survived – Christine Dohnanyi and Josef and Maria Müller. Otto John, who was in close touch with everyone involved at the time, has described what happened:

'Roeder in his investigations used methods which we at the time used to call Gestapo methods. I knew that not only from what Frau Dohnanyi and Frau Müller told me after their release, but also from what my friend Captain Gehre, and Dohnanyi himself told me . . . He put them under great mental pressure by threatening to persecute their wives if they did not make statements. I also remember the notes smuggled out of prison by Dohnanyi stating that Roeder would stop at nothing to get his way . . . Dohnanyi lived under constant threat that Roeder would hand him over to the Gestapo. I remember this very clearly because that would have led to Dohnanyi being tortured. None of us was under any illusion that subject to such appalling duress he might well be forced to make statements which could jeopardize the entire conspiracy against Hitler.

'Among those suffering anxiety that Dohnanyi might be handed over to the Gestapo were not only his wife but also General Oster, Dr Goerdeler and other members of the conspiracy. I recall this all so well because I could never get out of my mind what Dohnanyi had once told me shortly before his arrest when we were without friends: 'Not one of us really knows how long he can resist torture once they start doing their worst.' No wonder therefore that all Dohnanyi's friends did whatever they could to get him out of Roeder's clutches. What Roeder did constituted not only martyrdom for his victims but for their friends too.'

Everyone, from Canaris to Dr Karl Sack, head of the Military Judiciary, and even Colonel Otto Mass, Commandant of the Tegel prison, did what they could to ease the pressure on the prisoners. They resented the Gestapo's interference, since they were supposed, as security police, to be concerned solely with civilian investigations. Even Himmler was not enthusiastic about the Gestapo's involvement, and told Canaris he did not want them to take the case over. But Roeder had the bit between his teeth, and he accumulated sufficient evidence to keep the investigation alive. What worried Dohnanyi continually was that the contents of the underground safe at Zossen might be discovered. Smuggled messages began to pass between Dohnanyi and his wife, once she was released, which urged that Oster should have the papers removed and destroyed. In spite of assurances sent back, ostensibly in Oster's name (since he could do nothing) that this was being or would be done, the safe was never fully cleared – though it almost certainly was 'purged'. Many of the files belonging to the Resistance, including a typescript of the secret diary kept by Canaris, passed into the safe-keeping of Colonel Werner Schrader, the trusted member of the Resistance who was based at High Command headquarters at Zossen. Schrader hid the documents he removed in cases which he took to a farm near Brunswick belonging to his brother-in-law. These papers were destroyed by Frau Schrader after her husband's suicide following the failure of the attempt on Hitler's life in July 1944, and evidence given to Heinrich Fraenkel on this point appears in our book, *The Canaris Conspiracy*. The documents still kept at Zossen, however, were to remain secure for a while.

This was the position, therefore, during the hot summer months in Berlin when Tresckow, ostensibly on sick leave, developed more detailed plans for Hitler's assassination and an

**Count Peter Yorck von Wartenburg, a member of the Kreisau resistance circle**

Goerdeler, Olbricht, Tresckow and an important newcomer, Colonel Count Claus von Stauffenberg, a young man of thirty-six with extraordinary stamina and courage. He had a long record of anti-Nazism, and, like Oster, was often indiscreet about Hitler in the company of his fellow-officers, whether they shared his views or not. He was a friend of Tresckow, whom he had met when they were both staff-officers at General Stuelpnagel's headquarters in Paris after the fall of France. Stauffenberg, handsome and aristocratic, with a fearlessly idealistic Christian outlook, came from a family which had produced several distinguished men in the past. He could not bear the thought of Germany being ruled by Hitler.

Stauffenberg was not unknown to those aligned to the Resistance. He had exceptional knowledge, having served on both the Eastern and Western fronts as a staff officer. Just as Tresckow had tried to work on Kluge, so Stauffenberg had tried to work on General Fritz Erich von Manstein, Paulus's commander on the Eastern front at the time of the German collapse at Stalingrad. Manstein had refused to act against Hitler on the grounds that he was his Commander-in-Chief. Finally, while serving in Tunisia early in 1943, Stauffenberg was seriously wounded when his staff-car was attacked by low-flying aircraft. He underwent a series of critical operations, leaving him with only three fingers on his left hand and the complete loss of his right hand and forearm. His other injuries included the loss of his left eye. Any other man than Stauffenberg would have been invalided out of the Service. While convalescent he had told his wife that his sole ambition was to rid Germany of Hitler, and he arranged matters with Olbricht so that he might stay in the Reserve Army as a staff officer. He was attached to Olbricht's staff in October 1943, with a desk at the War Office on the Bendlerstrasse in Berlin. In fact, he

effective *coup*. Goerdeler tried to reach Churchill on behalf of the Resistance by sending a detailed memorandum via Sweden on the intentions of the post-Hitler government. Though the war was turning ever further against Hitler (the heavy air-raids penetrating as far inland as Berlin, the Allied invasion of Sicily and the fall of Mussolini in July 1943, the Allied invasion of Italy and the Italian surrender in September), it was a difficult period for the Resistance with Beck ill, both Canaris and Oster virtually inactive, and Dohnanyi confined. Another defeat for the Resistance was the arrests which followed penetration by a Gestapo agent into another circle of intellectual and diplomatic dissidents – the Solf group, centred round the widow of Dr Wilhelm Solf, former German ambassador in Japan, and Elizabeth von Thadden, a distinguished headmistress. They were friends of Moltke, and their arrest in the autumn of 1943 was eventually to lead to that of Moltke himself in January 1944.

The month of October 1943, saw renewed activity by the Resistance. Beck was somewhat recovered, and the inner corps centred now on Beck,

**Kaltenbrunner, Heydrich's successor as Head of Reich Security**

joined Tresckow, who was soon to return to the Eastern front, to put the final touches to the plan for the *coup d'état*. Kluge was still on sufficiently close terms with the Resistance to visit Olbricht and agree that assassination was the only way to remove Hitler so that some kind of negotiated peace could be conducted before Germany's inevitable collapse before the armies of the Soviet Union.

The plans for the *coup d'état* were given the code name of Valkyrie, and disguised as the operation necessary to cope on the home front with any mass revolt by the millions of slave workers based now on German soil. In particular it included the necessary troop movements by units of the home-based Reserve Army to occupy the administrative areas in Berlin. The Reserve Army by 1944 was made up largely of men whose age or physical condition made them unsuitable for service on the Eastern front. This was not the best material with which to face the formidable SS units, whose job was to maintain security and discipline in Germany. From the point of view of the Resistance, the position was constantly changing; commanding officers in Berlin who

were known to be potentially helpful were liable to be posted elsewhere and replaced by others who might prove less sympathetic in a state of emergency. But these were the risks those responsible for planning a *coup* had to take.

With the arrival of Stauffenberg and the subsequent, reluctant departure of Tresckow for the Eastern front, since he had been 'convalescent' for as long as he dared to be, the younger generation can be said to have assumed power. Though Stauffenberg gladly accepted the leadership of Beck, whom he liked and respected, he regarded Goerdeler as the originator of a 'revolution of greybeards'. Even Hassell regarded Goerdeler as 'something of a reactionary'. In any case, the men of the Resistance knew he was watched by the Gestapo. Goerdeler's reaction to Stauffenberg as a newcomer is interesting. He wrote that Stauffenberg:

'revealed himself as a cranky, obstinate fellow who wanted to play politics. I had many a row with him, but greatly esteemed him. He wanted to steer a dubious political course with the left-wing Socialists and the Communists, and gave me a bad time with his overwhelming egotism.'

Through sheer quality of personality and leadership, together with his remarkable capacity for overcoming the most daunting of war wounds, Stauffenberg gradually became the central figure in the Resistance as it came to be engineered largely by the younger generation. He was supported by Olbricht's more senior executive abilities, and guided sympathetically by the father-figure of Beck. But he undoubtedly wanted his own way. Gisevius speaks of him as 'a passionate soldier' who claimed, 'if not the right to political leadership, at least the prerogative of sharing in the political decisions.' He represented 'the new dynamism'.

And dynamism was what the Resistance had so far lacked – partly through sheer ill luck when the

enterprizing bomb plot of March 1943 had gone wrong, but mainly (though not entirely) because of the lack of ruthlessness in the men at the top, a ruthlessness which Stauffenberg managed to combine with his idealism. Had Kluge agreed to the arrest of Hitler the plot would most probably have succeeded. More than sheer courage was needed to unseat so all-powerful a dictator as Hitler. Courage was never lacking. For example, in November 1943 two young men volunteered in turn for suicide missions in order to assassinate Hitler. One was Baron Axel von dem Bussche, who was chosen to 'model' a new Army great-coat for the Führer. He put a bomb in the greatcoat pocket, but each time Hitler was due to see the coat the session was cancelled. Then, when Bussche was wounded in action, young Ewald von Kleist volunteered to replace him, though he was only twenty. His mission, too, came to nothing. Others who volunteered to attempt to shoot Hitler outright should he visit the Eastern front once again included Schlabrendorff himself. But the Führer never came.

The New Year brought another blow to the Resistance – the dismissal of Canaris from the Abwehr. The Abwehr was absorbed into Himmler's and Schellenberg's Intelligence service, the SD, and Canaris, though still not suspected of anything worse than incompetence and indiscretion, found that his movements were restricted, like those of Oster. What was lost to the Resistance as a result of this was not only Canaris's valuable support and advice, but the flow of important information which he could provide through the Abwehr. Dohnanyi, however, gained some temporary respite from prison; his health was deteriorating and he suffered injuries during an air-raid the previous November. For the best part of three months he was removed to the Charité hospital,

Fire fighting in Berlin under air attack
1943

where he was protected by Professor Sauerbruck and could be visited by his family and friends. But by mid-February 1944 he was confined again in the Buch military hospital. He was, however, spared interrogation, and his case was allowed to drift.

Stauffenberg's impatience expressed itself by turning to the Left for support. Though by upbringing a monarchist, he soon tired of the lack of response from the Western Allies which Trott was trying to achieve through Allen Dulles in Switzerland, and Goerdeler through his contacts in Sweden. Since the British and Americans chose to turn their backs on the Resistance, why not try the Russians? He was on terms of close friendship with men of the moderate, socialist Left such as Julius Leber and Wilhelm Leuschner, and he actually encouraged Leber to make contact with the Communist underground. He felt that spectacular action against Hitler should if possible be taken before the imminent invasion of northern Europe by the Western Allies. Much destruction and loss of life could be avoided, he felt, if the Germans could themselves secure the downfall of Hitler before the Allied landings made the negotiating position of Germany less favourable. Arrangements for a negotiated peace with Stalin might spike the guns which threatened from the West.

Meanwhile, plans for the assassination attempt on Hitler had to go forward. The problem as always was to get access to him. Another volunteer on the Eastern front was Colonel von Breitenbach, who offered to shoot Hitler during a staff conference, but found he could not get anywhere near enough to the Führer to secure a proper aim following a lightning draw. Hitler was surrounded on this occasion by a protective screen of SS men. Another staff officer, Major-General Stieff, the recipient of Tresckow's and Schlabrendorff's Cointreau bottles, who kept a small supply of British-made bombs at Rastenburg

89

Julius Leber, the German Socialist,
defendant at the Bomb Plot trial, 1944

for the use of the Resistance, suffered
the misfortune that they ignited
themselves and exploded under the
wooden tower where he had concealed
them. It was most fortunate that
Schrader, who, it will be remembered, was a loyal member of the
Resistance, was detailed to investigate this mysterious explosion, and
managed to hush the matter up until
it was forgotten. A new supply of
explosives had to be obtained, and
these were ready in time for the attempt of July 1944.

Then at last came a stroke of luck –
in June Stauffenberg was promoted
Chief of Staff to General Fromm,
Commander-in-Chief of the Reserve
Army. This meant that from time to
time he had to represent him at
Hitler's staff conferences, and this
gave him the coveted access to Hitler
at a time when he was least protected.
He stood in Hitler's presence for the
first time on 7th June 1944, the day
after the Allied landings in Normandy.
He looked Hitler in the eye and experienced none of the fear which so
many men in high places, including
even Göring and Himmler and the
generals of the High Command, undoubtedly felt, which made them

dread entering the presence of the
Führer in case they might have to
endure one of his fits of rage. When
Stauffenberg came back to Berlin he
knew that he must be the man to
carry the bomb into the Führer's
presence.

With his grave disabilities, the SS
did not stir themselves to check him
for concealed weapons. What could a
man with one eye and only three
fingers do to injure the Führer?
Stauffenberg was stirred by an in-
spiring message from Tresckow, chaf-
fing now in isolation on the Eastern
front:

'The assassination must be attempted, at any cost. Even should that fail,
the attempt to seize power in the
capital must be undertaken. We
must prove to the world and to future
generations that the men of the
German Resistance movement dared
to take the decisive step and to hazard
their lives upon it. Compared with
this, nothing else matters.'

Beck and Olbricht agreed. The need
for action became even more pressing
when Leber was arrested following his
meeting with the Communist underground representatives, of which the
Gestapo was aware. Details of the
handling of the news of Hitler's death
were also discussed with General
Erich Fellgiebel, Chief of Signals to
the Army, and a key man therefore at
this stage in the conspiracy, since he
could control the equipment by means
of which all announcements came
from Hitler's headquarters.

On 3rd July Stauffenberg had met
Stieff at Berchtesgaden, where Hitler
was stationed, and taken possession of
two bombs. His attendance at a staff
conference was next ordered for 11th
July, again at Berchtesgaden, and it
was agreed in Berlin that this should
be the day chosen for the attempt.
While Stauffenberg would be responsible for leaving the bomb on a
short time-fuse under Hitler's con-

Claus von Stauffenberg, a holiday
photograph of 1935

*Above:* The von Stauffenberg family: the Count and his sons (from left to right) Bertold, Claus and Alexander. *Right:* General von Manstein

ference table, Olbricht should take responsibility for putting Valkyrie into operation in Berlin on receiving a signal by telephone from Stauffenberg that all had gone well. But on the appointed day. Stauffenberg only signalled abandonment of the attempt, because neither Göring nor Himmler was present. At this stage the conspirators hoped to kill the more dangerous Nazi leaders as a group; Himmler, in particular, was dangerous because of his control of the Gestapo and SS. Then on 14th July Hitler without prior warning transferred himself and his staff north to Rastenburg, where his headquarters, known as the Wolf's Lair lay deep in the East Prussian forests.

Hitler called a further staff conference for 15th July, the day after his removal to Rastenburg, and Stauffenberg was ordered once again to be present. The conspirators had decided Olbricht should not put the Berlin forces of the Reserve Army on a Valkyrie alert on 11th July because they were uncertain in any case of success at the Berghof conference. They felt easier about conditions at Rastenburg, since Hitler normally called his conferences in a bomb-proof chamber – bomb-proof, that is, from explosions outside. It was decided in this instance that Olbricht should take the risk of putting the troops on alert at 11.00 hours, an hour before Hitler's conference, without Fromm's knowledge or authority. Fromm, in any case, was himself flying to Rastenburg. Fellgiebel in Rastenburg would signal Berlin if the attempt succeeded. Beck, a prey since his operation to nervous exhaustion, stayed in isolation at his small house in Lichterfeld, a suburb of Berlin, and Goerdeler went to keep him company until they were summoned, on the news of Hitler's death, to join Olbricht and his associates at the War Ministry in the Bendlerstrasse. Gisevius, who had been working as an agent for the Resistance on the German consular staff in Switzerland, had returned to Germany to join the conspirators.

One o'clock came, and then two o'clock – and there was still no news from Rastenburg. Stauffenberg, it transpired later, had been once again uncertain what to do, because Himmler and Göring were absent. He left the conference to put through a private call to Olbricht, and they agreed in veiled terms that Stauffenberg should make the attempt on Hitler alone. When he returned, however, he found the conference about to break up. Olbricht was in great difficulties to explain away, in terms of an exercise, the Valkyrie alert, for which he had to take personal responsibility. He was reprimanded by Fromm.

On 16th July Beck, Stauffenberg and Olbricht met again. The difficulties were discussed in the light of the fiasco of the previous day. The Valkyrie operation could not be ordered again unless Hitler was actually killed, and this was to inhibit the conspirators later, on the crucial 20th July. Nevertheless it was agreed that Hitler must be killed at the very next opportunity, if necessary alone among the Nazi hierarchy, but that Valkyrie must only be called after Fellgiebel's signal announcing the success of the attempt had been received.

Time was telling more and more against the conspirators. Kluge had been suddenly transferred to the Western front, and had left Tresckow behind him. On 17th July Rommel, the most popular general both with Hitler and the German public, but who favoured some curtailment of Hitler's powers, was lost to the Resistance when machine-gun fire fractured his

*Above left:* Fellgiebel, whose task in the plot was to block the Wolf's Lair signal circuits. *Above right:* Rommel, a victim of Hitler's retribution, July 1944. *Left:* Hitler walks in the woods at Rastenburg 1942

skull. Nevertheless, Stuelpnagel, Military Governor of France, stood firm by the Resistance, and was fully prepared to coordinate his actions in Paris with those of the conspirators in Berlin. Kluge, as always, remained an uncertain quantity.

On 18th July Stauffenberg had to warn Goerdeler to go into hiding, since his arrest was rumoured to be imminent. The threat was now great to Beck himself, indeed to everyone known to be watched by the Gestapo. Tension had reached breaking-point when Stauffenberg at last received his next summons to attend a Führer conference at Rastenburg.

The date of this conference was 20th July.

Stauffenberg was in his office as usual the day before, on 19th July. The secretary he shared with Olbricht, Delia Ziegler, one of the few women who knew the details of the conspiracy, understood only too well the dangers of his mission. Just before he left the office, Stauffenberg joked with her as he thrust another file into his briefcase, already bulging with the bomb, which was wrapped in an old

shirt. Stauffenberg had spent the day on the routine work of preparing his situation report for Hitler, who was deeply concerned about the penetration of the Russian armies to the very borders of the Poland of 1939. Stauffenberg must have thought at this time of everyone in the intimate circle of the Resistance who now depended upon him – of Dohnanyi, Müller and Bonhoeffer confined in prison, of Beck in his state of exhaustion but eager to take his place at the head of the new government, of Canaris, Goerdeler and Oster, living day by day in the deep shadow of suspicion, and of the tens of thousands dying each day on the battlefronts and in the genocide and labour camps. He must have thought of his wife, the Countess Nina, who was living away from Berlin at their country estate at Lautlingen in southern Germany. She was three months pregnant.

On his way to his rooms, he stopped his staff car outside a Catholic church in Dahlem. He went in and prayed for the success of his enterprise, on which the restoration of peace and some new measure of justice in Europe depended

# 20th July 1944

Hitler passes the guard house at the
outermost ring of the Rastenburg
defences

Stauffenberg woke early in the bedroom loaned him in the house belonging to a relative in Wannsee. It was already hot. He shaved and dressed, using his three fingers with astonishing deftness. Since his recovery he had insisted on being as independent of outside help as possible. The staff car due to take him and his young adjutant, Lieutenant Werner von Haeften, to Rangsdorf Airport was due to arrive at six o'clock. Haeften was as eager for success in the attempt that day as Stauffenberg. He would be carrying a second briefcase and in it. was a second bomb with which, if the first for any reason failed, it might be possible to continue the operation.

The car arrived promptly, and Haeften saw Stauffenberg and the briefcase safely bestowed. They drove to the airport where Stieff, the officer on Hitler's staff whose charge on behalf of the Resistance had been to care for the small stock of bombs, was waiting to join them in the flight north. Before Stauffenberg had volunteered Stieff himself had been regarded as the man who might place the bomb. The Countess Nina Stauffenberg still believed this, and her husband had not thought it wise to disillusion her. But Stieff, it would appear, had lost some of his nerve during the long period of delay and tension. Stauffenberg faced his mission with an air of calmness, even of gaiety. He did not fear Hitler.

The flight to Rastenburg occupied almost three hours in the slow staff plane, a Heinkel, allocated to Stieff and Stauffenberg by General Wagner of Zossen, who also knew what was afoot. They touched down around ten o'clock, and the pilot was instructed to have the aircraft ready for an immediate take-off at any time after mid-day. The rest of the journey was a short run by car of about nine miles along the country road into the forests which concealed the Wolf's Lair.

Entry to the innermost section of the Lair necessitated passing through three successive check-points under SS control. Hitler's headquarters, sunless and overshadowed by tall, encircling trees, were protected by minefields and wire fencing, some of it electrified. Here is was that Hitler, poring over his large-scale maps, plotted the movements of his armies with a strategy determined by the information either given or slanted or withheld by his staff officers.

The SS men at the check-points required to see the special passes carried by Stauffenberg and Haeften. This was normal at headquarters. For Stauffenberg and Haeften to get inside was easy – they had the necessary documents. But to get out after the explosion was, they knew, going to be a test of both speed and nerve. With Hitler gone, Stauffenberg would be urgently needed in Berlin to lend his energy and skill to the achievement of the *coup d'état*.

Hitler's conference had in fact been called for one o'clock, so there was time to kill. However, Stauffenberg had to have a word with Fellgiebel, though it was well understood that his contribution to the day was to give Olbricht the message that the mission was accomplished and then, as Chief of Signals, to shut down all communications between Rastenburg and the outside world. With Hitler dead and his headquarters cut off from all independent contact, the *coup* could proceed rapidly in Berlin. The troops would move in to deal with any trouble in the administrative sector of the city, and Beck, assuming temporary command on behalf of the new government, would announce the fact of Hitler's death over the radio to the German public and the peoples of the world.

Only Stieff and Fellgiebel knew anything of what was planned to take place that day at Rastenburg. Stauffenberg met Fellgiebel after having breakfasted with Haeften. He then went over to pay a formal visit to Field-Marshal Keitel, Hitler's Chief of Staff. He found Keitel anxious to see him. Hitler had decided to hold his conference half an hour earlier, at

Hofacker, a leading conspirator in the German headquarters in France 1944

12.30 hours, since Mussolini, Italy's deposed dictator who was now little more than Hitler's dependent, was expected to visit Rastenburg at 14.30 hours that afternoon. Reports must be kept brief. Stauffenberg was momentarily anxious; how far might this new arrangement affect conditions at the conference? Would the attempt once again have to be abandoned? He decided the change of time need have little effect; the assassination would take place half an hour earlier, that was all.

Back in Berlin, Olbricht sat at his desk trying to pass the morning with routine business. He expected Fellgiebel's signal not later than 13.30 hours. Then he would immediately summon Beck to the Ministry and put the full Valkyrie operation into effect. This would lead, as soon as the troops arrived, to the occupation of the Ministries, the radio stations, and other centres, and the immobilisation of the SS. The War Office had telegraphic communication with every Commander on the battlefronts, and further signals could go out as soon as Beck was prepared to authorize them. A factor on the side of the conspirators was that Rastenburg could only make contact with the rest of the Army through the communications system at the Ministry. Meanwhile General Hoepner (whom Hitler had dismissed for incompetence) was due to arrive later in the morning to help Olbricht, while General Wagner at Command headquarters at Zossen stood by to assist. General Count Wolf von Helldorf, President of the Berlin Police, a previous supporter of Hitler who had turned against him, was holding a force of his own men in reserve.

The success of the Valkyrie plan depended a great deal upon shock – the shock of Hitler's death bringing all the Army commanders and their forces over to the conspirators' aid so that order might be maintained. It was, in effect, to be a military *coup d'état* establishing a caretaker government in which prominent civilians would be included. Stauffenberg was expected back during the later afternoon, and a small number of younger officers who enjoyed the confidence of the conspirators were standing by to assist when called upon to do so. Certain secretaries, led by Olbricht's and Stauffenberg's principal secretary, Delia Ziegler, were also briefed to help administratively. As we have seen, women had on the whole been excluded from sharing in the detailed knowledge of the plan because of its enormous dangers, but some few at the War Ministry had to be let into the conspirators' secrets, along with certain of the wives of the men principally involved.

In Paris, the only commanding general directly involved was Stuelpnagel. He too was surrounded by a group of young officers anxious to help in the *coup d'état*, especially Cäsar von Hofacker, who was Stauffenberg's cousin. Stuelpnagel's headquarters were in the Majestic Hotél on the Avenue Kléber; this was the equivalent centre in Paris to the War Ministry in Berlin, which was usually referred to by the name of the street in which its was situated, namely the Bendlerstrasse. But whereas General

*Above:* Stieff (smiling, centre) the guardian of the conspirators' bombs. *Below:*
Hitler, Brauchitsch and Raeder at the Rastenburg map table

Fromm, Olbricht's and Stauffenberg's Commander, was in the same building as themselves and was unlikely to offer them his support unless the success of the *coup* was very apparent, Stuelpnagel knew that his Commander, Kluge, was inclined to prove helpful once he was assured others had completed the dirty part of the work. But Kluge's headquarters were situated in La Roche-Guyon, at some distance from Paris. In Paris, Stuelpnagel was in charge of the plans for the *coup*. But for the moment all he could do was wait for the long-hoped-for signal from Berlin telling him to proceed with his carefully prepared action against the chief officers of the SS and Gestapo.

Gisevius went over to Helldorf's office during the morning. Like the others he found it difficult to kill time. By now the day was really oppressive, alike in Rastenburg and Berlin. There was thunder in the air. It entertained them, however, when a nervous young officer arrived from the War Ministry with a map of the buildings to be occupied. Helldorf studied it, and then demanded cynically to know why the Army men who had prepared it had used a map long out-of-date which made no allowance for the effects of recent bombing. Some of the places marked for occupation had been destroyed. Helldorf was irritated because the Army seemed to think that, given this map, he would be prepared to act on his own initiative. He insisted that the Army conspirators were the planners of the whole enterprise, and that they must therefore act first. Once their forces had surrounded the administrative area, he would throw in his men to help them, but not before.

So while Stauffenberg, Stieff and Fellgiebel, together with Haeften, waited for the 12.30 conference at Rastenburg, Olbricht waited at the War Ministry, Beck at his home in the suburbs of Berlin, and Stuelpnagel at the Majestic in Paris. At about 12.30 (half an hour before the time the conference was thought by those away from Rastenburg to begin), General Hoepner arrived at the War Ministry. He was dressed in civilian clothes, but he was carrying a small suitcase in which his uniform was packed. He was to act as Commander of the Reserve Army should Fromm prove hostile to the enterprise. He announced himself as having an appointment with Olbricht; he was checked in at the Reception desk and taken to Olbricht's office. Anxious to avoid suspicion by not taking lunch as usual, Olbricht invited Hoepner over to the officer's club for a hasty meal, from which they fully expected to be summoned by phone by Fraulein Ziegler, Olbricht's secretary, when the signal from Rastenburg came through. They drank to the success of the *coup*, and to the assassination they believed was soon to take place.

But they were not interrupted at their meal. When they had finished, they hurried back to the office. Their eyes were on the clock, and their ears strained for the sound of the telephone. But no call came. Perhaps it occurred to them how frail the link was on which they were so completely dependent. But they could do nothing until the telephone rang. A telephone standing silent on a desk can seem singularly incommunicative. It takes two people, otherwise entirely cut off from each other, to make a telephone active. Already that morning, in Paris, a telephone had acted mysteriously. Colonel Finckh, a member of Kluge's staff and stationed on the Rue de Surène, received a call the exact origin of which was never traced; when he lifted the receiver an unnamed voice, announced as speaking from Zossen, hesitated momentarily and then uttered the single word, 'Exercise'. Finckh heard the instrument click as it was replaced without further explanation. Finckh was involved to a limited extent in Stuelpnagel's plans and understood, therefore, what the word might signify. Indeed on 15th July, the

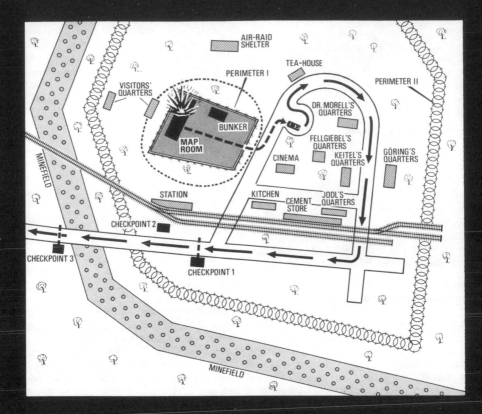

**Rastenburg: the Wolf's Lair**

**General Stülpnagel, central figure of the conspiracy in Paris**

same code word had been telephoned through. Feeling uneasy, however, about the lack of any identification on this occasion, Finckh reported this 'incident' to Hofacker, who, as we have seen was one, of Stuelpnagel's more intimate associates in the conspiracy. They had certainly not been led to expect any order of this kind so soon, or delivered in this enigmatic manner. They could only assume it was meant to put them on the alert. Finckh's uneasiness was all the stronger because he was one of those officers who stood slightly aloof from the conspiracy, since he did not approve of Hitler's assassination.

It was coming up to 12.30. Stauffenberg, in order to play for time and gain a moment to himself, had left his cap and belt in the ante-room. Keitel chaffed at this delay; naturally, Hitler did not like to be kept waiting. Stauffenberg made his excuses, put on his belt, opened his briefcase, and activated the bomb, as he had trained himself to do, his three fingers operating a pair of tweezers. The bomb was on a ten-minute fuse, the shortest time possible. Stauffenberg had a three-minute walk across the compound and then seven minutes in

which to enter Hitler's presence, deposit the briefcase as near to him as possible, make a hurried excuse about taking a phone call from Berlin, and escape. Haeften was waiting nearby with the staff car and driver – and the reserve bomb ready to use if the first failed.

The conference was taking place in a large wooden building lightly reinforced with concrete and known as the Operations or Map Room, or sometimes simply as the Conference Room. This was unlucky. Had there been an alert, the meeting would have had to be transferred to one of the concrete bunkers normally used for the purpose. It was very humid and airless in this place surrounded by trees, and as Stauffenberg hurried over to the conference, which he knew would have already started by now, he wondered how far the effectiveness of the bomb would be diminished. He entered the building strode down its corridor past the telephonist's room, and entered the relatively bare Conference Room, at the further end of which Hitler was standing. His attention was rivetted on a large scale map of the Eastern front which virtually covered the table in front of him. Round this extensive table were grouped some twenty staff officers, but neither Himmler nor Göring was among them. Stauffenberg eased himself into the meeting as inconspicuously as he could, moving close to Hitler.

He took in the situation in a second with his single eye. The windows in the wall on the further side of the table were thrown wide open, for the room was stiflingly hot. It was some eighteen feet by forty, with the table near the line of windows. With these windows wide open, the effect of the blast was bound to be greatly diminished. The bomb had to be placed as near to Hitler as possible.

Everyone was listening intently to a pessimistic report on the situation on the Eastern front given by General Heusinger, Chief of Operations. More reserves were needed. It was a most dangerous moment for Stauffenberg; he might have been called upon to give his report on the reserves available while the acid ate through the last shreds of the filament of the wire in the time-fuse. But Hitler, fortunately, wanted the report on the position completed first. Stauffenberg slipped his heavy-looking briefcase to the ground, lodging it almost at Hitler's feet, leaning against one of the heavy wooden plinths supporting the table over which Hitler was leaning. Murmuring his excuses about the phone call from Berlin, he ignored any attempt which might be made by Keitel or anyone else to keep him in the meeting and strode out, walking as fast as he could past the telephonists' room, down the corridor, and out into the humid air. He passed uninterrupted through the checkpoint of the innermost control and hurried across the compound – a distance in all of some hundreds of yards – to the place near Fellgiebel's office where Haeften was waiting by the staff car. Fellgiebel stood with him. They were watching Stauffenberg approach them, counting the seconds for the bomb to go off. The ten minutes must be virtually exhausted. Seeing Stauffenberg had almost completed the walk, Haeften got into the car. The engine was already running.

As Stauffenberg reached the staff car, the explosion went off with an enormous, deafening sound. Stauffenberg knew at once from its sheer magnitude that his mission must have been successful. It was 12.42 by their watches – the historic moment (he was convinced) of Hitler's death. Leaving Fellgiebel to contact Berlin, there was not a moment to lose for Stauffenberg and Haeften to escape from the Wolf's Lair. There were the two remaining check-points to negotiate, and the guards would have heard the explosion.

The staff car raced round the circuit to the first check-point, and stopped. Stauffenberg jumped out, demanded use of the telephone, called the Duty Officer, and exercised his authority to clear his right of exit – without the guard himself speaking to the Officer. His departure time was logged as 12.44 hours. At the last checkpoint he tried to use the same procedure. He was unlucky; the SS sergeant in charge refused to accept Stauffenberg's account of what the Duty Officer had said. By now orders had been given that no one was to pass out without exceptional authority. Stauffenberg resorted to the telephone again, and was most fortunate that the Duty Officer gave the sergeant instruction to let him leave. He was, after all, a senior officer from headquarters in Berlin, and, with his injuries, something of a national hero. He could not be suspect.

Haeften and he were clear at last of the Wolf's Lair. The car, driven at full speed, tore along the road to the airport. Haeften opened his briefcase, took out the second bomb, dismantled it into segments, and threw them joyously piece by piece into the cover of the trees and bushes through which they were passing. Who was there to care now Hitler was gone?

The plane was ready for them. They hurried aboard, and took off for Berlin at 13.15 hours. The *coup d'état* was on!

As soon as Stauffenberg's car had left, Fellgiebel had run towards the conference building from which the explosion had come. Everyone thought a bomb had fallen from a lone Russian plane which had sneaked in low without warning, dropping the bomb with pin-point precision. That was what Hitler believed as he staggered out of the wrecked building, supported by Keitel. Hitler was the first person Fellgiebel saw as he arrived on the scene. He was horrified. What was he to signal to Berlin?

With the windows wide open and the table-top acting as a shield, most of the men in the conference room had escaped without serious injury. Each of the survivors was later to give his own account of what had happened to the SS investigators. In the main

# PRINCIPAL PERSONS PRESENT IN THE MAP ROOM AT 12.42pm 20th JULY 1944

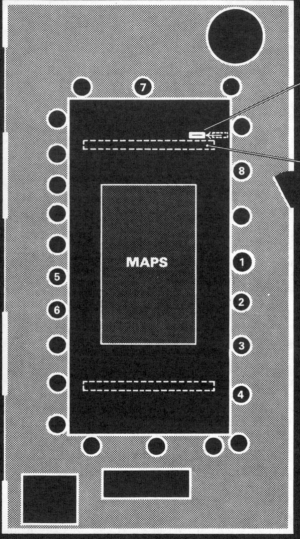

BRIEF-CASE BOMB, PUSHED FURTHER UNDER TABLE BY COLONEL BRANDT

HEAVY SUPPORT SHIELDS HITLER FROM WORST OF BLAST

1  Hitler

2  Field-Marshal Keitel, Chief of German Armed Forces High Command (OKW)

3  Colonel-General Jodl, Chief of OKW Operations Staff

4  General Warlimont, Deputy Chief of OKW Operations Staff

5  Rear Admiral Voss, representative of Grand-Admiral Raeder at Hitler's HQ

6  SS-Gruppenführer Fegelein, representative of the Waffen-SS at Hitler's HQ

7  General Schmundt, Chief Adjutant of the OKW to Hitler

8  Colonel-General Korten, Chief of the Luftwaffe General Staff

these recollections coincided, though they might differ in points of detail.

Some seemed to remember that Colonel Brandt, Heusinger's Chief of Staff, edging nearer to the table beside Hitler to study the vast large-scale map spread out before them, had kicked a bulging briefcase which was in the way of his feet, and had bent down and moved it to the other side of the table's plinth. It had been Stauffenberg's briefcase. The bomb, therefore, had exploded with the heavy wooden plinth acting as a powerful shield; its full force was prevented from reaching the Führer. In his place, it killed Brandt, the man who had moved it, and three others – General Korten, chief of the General Staff of the Luftwaffe, General Schmundt, chief adjutant of the Armed Forces, and a stenographer called Berger. Two others, General Bodenschatz of the Luftwaffe and Colonel Bergmann, one of Hitler's adjutants, were severely injured; all the rest either escaped injury or were slightly hurt, and suffering from shock. Hitler himself escaped without severe injury. At the time of the explosion he had been virtually lying on the table, stretched out to his fullest extent as he peered at a distant area of the map – the north-east area showing the Kurland district. The table, as well as the plinth which supported it, had protected the vital parts of his body. Keitel, who was uninjured, had managed to stagger over the debris and help him to his feet. He had led him out, and helped him reach his private accommodation, little more than a hundred feet away.

As the pair of them had emerged from the wreck of the wooden building Fellgiebel had seen that Hitler's hair was singed and smoking. On examination, it was found that the Führer's right arm was partly paralysed, his right leg – the one nearer to the bomb – badly burned, his ear-drums damaged, and his buttocks bruised so that, as he put it himself, he had a 'backside like a baboon'. His first reaction, apparently, was anger that his trousers, which were new, had been ruined; the blast had ripped them from top to bottom, the tears being so neat they might have been slit with a tailor's shears.

Hitler's second reaction was to order SS Security to close down all communication with the outside world until this event had been fully investigated. No one must learn of this near successful attempt on his life. Fellgiebel, who knew Stauffenberg was on his way back to Berlin convinced that Hitler was dead, hurried back to his office to make some kind of signal to his friends in Berlin that everything had gone wrong, but expressed in terms which would not arouse suspicion at this most difficult time. He found that his Signals Sector was already under the control of the SS. No messages, he learned, were to be sent out without Hitler's express authorization. He was helpless. Stieff, he found, thought that any idea of a *coup* should be abandoned at once, now that Hitler was still alive. In his view, each of the conspirators should do nothing now but protect himself and his colleagues.

Hitler, meanwhile, had summoned Himmler, as head of the SS, to take charge of the investigations into the event, which he still considered to be the result of a plane penetrating the security screen. Himmler, whose own headquarters were only some twenty-five kilometres away on the lake of Maursee, was driven in haste to Rastenburg with his bodyguard Kiermaier beside him; the journey took only half an hour in spite of the indifferent roads. Stauffenberg was barely half way to Berlin in his slow aircraft before Himmler and the SS investigators were beginning their interrogations. Himmler also ordered certain experts to fly at once from Berlin. Meanwhile, with Keitel's knowledge of Stauffenberg's strange behaviour, it did not take long to establish that the bomb had not fallen from the air and that the man most

**Shaken and huddled in a cloak, Hitler returns to the scene of the assassination attempt. Himmler is beside him, Mussolini and Göring behind**

likely to have planted it was that young colonel with one eye and no right arm, who had left the conference in such a hurry and had not been seen again. The times he had checked out at each control point had been duly logged.

Hitler, with the instincts of a good propagandist still alive in him, determined to receive Mussolini during the later afternoon, when a state tea-party had been arranged after the former Duce had arrived by train. A branch line ran directly into the heart of the Rastenburg complex. The Führer was calm now and convinced, in his mystical way, that his life was charmed. He considered his escape to have been miraculous, a certain sign that Providence was on his side, and that he was preserved to lead Germany to an eventual victory, an illusion he was always to maintain in spite of the most serious reverses. This was his determined reaction to the attempt which had failed. The fact that Mussolini's private train was subjected to delay gave him further time to recover from the shock of the explosion, and so set an example to the others at his headquarters.

Back in Berlin, the afternoon was advancing with no signal of any kind from Rastenburg to guide the conspirators waiting in the Ministry on the Bendlerstrasse. The only person in Berlin to be given the bare facts that an explosion had taken place was Joseph Goebbels. He had been told this (but no more) around one o'clock, at the same time as the other senior ministers – Himmler, Göring and Ribbentrop. Goebbels on 20th July was the only one of the Nazi hierarchy in Berlin. The rest were in, or like Himmler, near to Rastenburg. Goebbels, though he did not yet know it, was the only responsible Nazi leader to be stationed in the place where the *coup* was planned to originate, and even he knew nothing of Hitler's personal involvement and escape until a subsequent message was relayed to him later.

As for the conspirators themselves, they remained completely in the dark. Their anxiety was intense. A slender shred of information reached Gisevius with tantilising incompleteness. When he and Helldorf could bear the uncertainty no longer, they took the risk of initiating a telephone call to their friend Arthur Nebe, the head of the German Criminal Investigation Department and, like Helldorf, a sympathiser with the conspiracy. Nebe was supposed to have telephoned Helldorf should he, by any chance, have received his own independent information from Rastenburg. All Nebe managed to gather during the early afternoon, around two o'clock, was that there had been some sort of explosion at the Wolf's Lair, and that Himmler had ordered SS investigators to leave Berlin at once to initiate enquiries on the spot. Hitler's name was never mentioned. Nebe did not dare to say even this much on the phone; here merely muttered that 'something strange has happened in East Prussia', and, with astonishing inefficiency, Gisevius and Nebe, who arranged to meet so that they might speak privately, mistook their rendezvous, and wasted further precious time waiting for each other in different places.

The telephone, with its hints and half-truths, continued to act as the primary vehicle of incommunication. In Paris, too, a further mysterious phone call reached Finckh around two o'clock in the form of another personal call from Zossen. The same anonymous voice that had spoken before uttered another single word – '*Abgelaufen;* launched! The word was repeated, and then before Finckh could speak himself, the caller replaced his receiver with a click.

Finckh observed his schedule of instructions exactly – given this signal to start the *coup* in France, he was to drive at once to General Staff headquarters of the Western Command, which was outside Paris, and report finally to Kluge's Chief of Staff,

General Blumentritt, that a *coup d'état* was 'launched'. Since Blumentritt was not involved in the conspiracy, only the simple facts could be given him. So on his arrival in Blumentritt's presence a little after three o'clock in the afternoon, Finckh, quite unconscious he was the first man to utter these memorable, if wholly incorrect words, stood rather nervously before the large and friendly figure of Blumentritt and said, 'Herr General. There has been a Gestapo *putsch* in Berlin. The Führer is dead. A provisional government has been formed by Generals Witzleben and Beck and Dr Goerdeler.'

Blumentritt paused to take in this news. He remained quite calm. Then he said he was glad these particular men were in charge because they would sue for peace. No one on the Western front was under much illusion the way things were going after the Normandy landings six weeks before, and the situation in the East did not bear contemplation. Naturally, however, Blumentritt questioned Finckh about the source of his news. Finckh took a risk and gave a prepared answer, 'The Military Governor', that is, Stuelpnagel; he had to assume Stuelpnagel, as head of the conspiracy in Paris, must have been informed at the same time as himself, if not before; no one, including Stuelpnagel, used the telephone if it could be helped, since all phones must be assumed to be tapped by the Gestapo.

Blumentritt quietly accepted Finckh's statement without further question. He put in a priority call to Field-Marshal Kluge, his commanding officer, and Army Group Commander in France. He could reach only Speidel, Kluge's Chief of Staff, who told him Kluge was away, touring the battlefronts, and would not be back until evening. Since Blumentritt also feared the ears of the Gestapo, he became nervous what to say next when Speidel began to press him. He therefore used defensive suggestion, and said, 'Things are happening in Berlin', and then risked adding the word, 'Dead' in a whisper. This only left Speidel the more mystified. Had Stuelpnagel been told the same thing, he would have been only a little the wiser. The conspirators in Berlin did not make contact with him until four-thirty to tell him Hitler must be considered dead, and that the *coup* in Germany had been launched. Stuelpnagel was delighted, and put his own plans in action at once.

This news was conveyed to him as a result of the desperate decisions which had been reached in the Ministry in Berlin during the mid-afternoon. Only at three-thirty had communications with Rastenburg been momentarily opened up. General Fritz Thiele, Olbricht's Signals Officer, managed to penetrate the silence at the Wolf's Lair, and received a garbled, nervously worded response to his question. This was, merely, that an attempt had been made on Hitler's life. No more, no less. No information whether Hitler was alive or dead. He hurried to Olbricht's office with the news.

If the *coup* was to be successful, Olbricht knew it must be launched with the least possible delay. The forces supporting Hitler must be given as little chance as possible to rally to the Nazi government of the Third Reich.

Olbricht faced a grave dilemma. Had Stauffenberg been successful? It sounded now as if he might have been – how account otherwise for the strange behaviour at Rastenburg? According to Oster's calculations, the bomb could not have exploded earlier than 13.15 hours – for it must be remembered he knew nothing of the change of time of the staff conference. Stauffenberg, if he had escaped, could not be expected back at Berlin's Rangsdorf airport before 16.45 at the earliest, if not 17.00 hours. He at least would bring them the truth, if he came at all. But to leave the Valkyrie operation unlaunched until then would probably be fatal to the success of the *coup*;

**Göring inspects the devastated interior
of the conference room**

for all he knew, counteraction might
already have been ordered. Olbricht,
in fact, carried the main responsibility
for initiating and organizing the *coup*,
just as Stauffenberg carried the responsibility for the assassination; he
had only Hoepner to advise him, and
Hoepner was by now distinctly nervous and cautious. By 15.45 hours
Olbricht felt he must take all their
lives in his hands and make a decision.
Once again, without consulting
Fromm, who was only a matter of
yards away from him at the Ministry,
Olbricht decided to send out the
Valkyrie signals. They began to go
out to the various commands of the
Reserve Army at 15.50. By 16.00 hours
several commands had received them,
either by telephone or teleprinter. But
it took time. They only reached
Vienna at 16.45 hours.

At around 16.00 hours Stauffenberg
touched down at Rangsdorff, half an
hour earlier than expected. There was
another hitch; no staff car was waiting
to bring him and Haeften to the Ministry. They anxiously telephoned the
Bendlerstrasse. It was then that they
learned the Valkyrie signals were only
just going out, and that Fellgiebel had
never telephoned. Stauffenberg was
dismayed; forgetting the needs of
security, he declared, 'Hitler is dead!'.
He commandeered a staff car at Rangsdorf, and left at full speed to join his
colleagues at the Ministry.

Heartened by the sound of Stauffenberg's voice and this assurance that
the Führer was indeed dead, Olbricht
decided he would now put the position
bluntly to Fromm, whom he knew
would only join in the conspiracy if it
was absolutely certain it would be in
his interest to do so, and that Hitler
was out of the way. Fromm listened
grimly and suspiciously to what
Olbricht had to say, then asked him
on what authority he had obtained
this news. On the authority of Fellgiebel, said Olbricht, Hitler was dead.

In the circumstances, added Olbricht firmly, he proposed to issue the code signals for Valkyrie to all Reserve Army Commands.

But Fromm was utterly opposed to being so precipitate. He declared that before he was prepared to let the signals go out, he wanted proper confirmation from Keitel. Olbricht with Stauffenberg's joyful words fresh in his ears, and believing in any case a response from Rastenburg on the telephone was impossible, put in a 'blitz' priority call. He was astonished when Fromm was almost immediately connected with Keitel.

'What's been happening at General Headquarters?' asked Fromm. 'There are wild rumours here in Berlin.'

'What do they say's happening?' countered Keitel. 'Everything is normal here.'

'I've had a report the Führer's been assassinated,' declared Fromm.

'Nonsense,' replied Keitel. 'It's true an attempt's been made on his life. Fortunately, it failed. The Führer's alive and was only slightly injured. But where's your Chief of Staff, Stauffenberg?'

'Stauffenberg's not back yet', said Fromm.

When the call was finished, Fromm told Olbricht curtly that there was certainly no need for the Valkyrie signals. Olbricht was stunned by what he had heard. He could only assume Keitel was lying. He retired from the room in some embarrassment, leaving Fromm to discover for himself in due time that the Valkyrie orders had already gone out. The *coup* had to continue. Above all, Olbricht needed to confer with Stauffenberg the moment he arrived. Beck, too, and Witzleben should also be here at any moment, and they could deal with Fromm.

As soon as Olbricht got back to his room – which became, for the moment, the headquarters of the *coup* – everyone concerned in the conspiracy in Berlin seemed to arrive at once – Beck, looking drawn and anxious, though resolute now that the testing

time had at last come, and above all Stauffenberg, dashing in with Haeften, both excited and eager for action. The winds of liberation blew through the musty offices of the Bendlerstrasse, and the torpor born of the humidity and the anxious hours of waiting through the afternoon were immediately dispersed. The younger generation of officers also converged on Olbricht's office to offer their help and to listen to Haeften's story of Rastenburg – Ewald von Kleist, Hans Fritzsche, von Hammerstein and von Oppen; they had been waiting in the Esplanade Hotel restaurant nearby for their summons. Witzleben, however, who was to assume command of the Armed Forces as a whole, was not to arrive until seven-thirty; Beck became very concerned at his continued absence. Stauffenberg telephoned personally to give the glad news of Hitler's death to Stuelpnagel's office in Paris; he spoke to Stuelpnagel's aide, Hofacker, and told him Stuelpnagel could rest assured he should proceed against the leaders of the SS and Gestapo, his primary task at this stage. Then Helldorf and Gisevius arrived. 'So we're off!', cried Helldorf. He was encouraged. Stauffenberg at least seemed to radiate energy.

Beck was uneasy about Keitel's assertions that Hitler was still alive and well in Rastenburg. 'But he's obviously lying,' Olbricht went on insisting. But Beck wanted these doubts to be taken into account, and stressed that Helldorf should, in all fairness, know of them. Beck surmised that Keitel's line would be that taken by the Nazi leaders when announcements, if any, were made. Rastenburg would have to take some counter-action now that the orders establishing a *coup d'état* were going out to commands everywhere, including Paris and Vienna. But Stauffenberg opposed any doubts that Hitler was dead. Had he not *heard* him die? Indeed, seen the smoke rising from the explosion?

'I saw the whole thing myself,' he

Göring and Himmler were among the first who arrived to re-affirm their loyalty

**Kluge, Commander of Army Group B in Normandy**

asserted. 'I was standing with Fellgiebel. It was just as if a 150mm shell had hit the barracks. It's impossible for anyone to have survived.'

Beck was naturally prepared to accept Stauffenberg's word; what concerned him deeply was any attempt which might be made by the opposition to pretend that Hitler was still alive, and so confuse the issue with the armed forces and the German public. This could well lead to doubts and difficulties which might be crucial for the outcome of the *coup*. He was worried, too, at the very late start to the operation. Most units on which they depended had some distance to travel to reach the centre of Berlin; at best it would be early evening, between five and six o'clock, before they could be effective. Meanwhile the Ministries and such vital centres of control as the broadcasting stations remained unoccupied by supporters of the Resistance. Gisevius, in particular, was worried that the broadcasting stations had not been taken over from the start. Beck's initial message to the German people should, in his view, have been broadcast by now. And then there was Fromm, an obvious source of danger in

the War Ministry itself. Gisevius considered that if he would not join them, he should be shot. Stauffenberg swept aside any such suggestions. At five o'clock, when the Valkyrie orders were safely out, and the units (it was hoped) well on their way into Berlin, Stauffenberg and Olbricht, supported by Kleist and Haeften, went to beard Fromm in his room in order to demand a show-down.

Meanwhile something approaching a ceremony was taking place in Rastenburg. It was as if a pilgrimage of the Nazi leaders had taken place in order to celebrate their Führer's deliverance from death – Himmler, Göring, Ribbentrop, Doenitz, everyone of special note, in fact, except Goebbels, who remained in Berlin, though he kept in telephonic touch with Rastenburg. At four o'clock Hitler stood ready on the railway platform inside the Wolf's Lair to receive Mussolini's private train. He was determined to make the most of his escape. He made the Duce's eyes bulge with his story of the bomb, and his appearance certainly confirmed what he had to say. He stood in the heat, threatening now to turn to misty rain amid the trees, a protective cloak clasped round him. His face was white, his arm in a sling, and he had cotton wool stuffed into his damaged ears. His burnt hair had been clipped and tidied. But he was elated, and hastened to take his guest to see the wrecked conference room and show him the singed remains of his uniform, Mussolini, whose own downfall was complete, had to be witness to the Führer's magic survival.

'Heaven has held its protective hand over you,' he said solemnly. Then they left to discuss the rather less miraculous situation on the battlefronts. At five o'clock they and their entourages took their places for tea, which was served by white-gloved menservants of the SS.

By now Himmler's investigations were beginning to clarify the situation. His experts were on their way from Berlin; their plane, in fact, crossed with that carrying Stauffenberg to Berlin. Until late in the afternoon Himmler and the SS officers working with him on the spot were convinced that the attempt had been no more than the mad act of an individual officer, whom they identified with the much-wounded Stauffenberg. Himmler telephoned and ordered Stauffenberg's arrest if not at the airport, then at the Bendlerstrasse. SS Colonel Piffraeder's car had crossed on its way to Rangsdorf with that of Stauffenberg on his way to the Bendlerstrasse.

When the outpour of Valkyrie orders was discovered at Rastenburg late in the afternoon, it became plain that there was more to the outrage than an attempt by a lone man to kill the Führer. Before sitting down to tea, Hitler told Himmler to leave the investigations at Rastenburg to his subordinates. His presence was needed in Berlin; he should take charge of the situation as it seemed to be developing there. Suspicious that Fromm was in some way involved, Hitler created Himmler Commander-in-Chief of the Reserve Army in Fromm's place – thus fulfilling the SS Reichsführer's lifelong ambition to have an

**General Schmundt, Hitler's Army adjutant, killed at his side**

army command. Himmler had always wanted to be a soldier; now suddenly at teatime on 20th July, he had become a Commander-in-Chief without a single day's service on a field of battle to his credit or a single year in the Army, even in his callow youth.

The teaparty which followed turned into a madhouse. At the centre table sat Hitler with his principal guests, vying with each other to pay their tributes to the great leader and curse all those officers who, if they were not actively plotting to assassinate him, were stabbing him in the back by crumbling before his victorious enemies on the battlefronts. One by one they assured him in turn that their hearts, at least, were in the right place, and that the Party and the nation were solidly behind him. Then, in what must be regarded as the hysterical release of the moment, these men, none of whom had in fact been present at the time of the explosion, fell into mutual recrimination – Doenitz against Göring, Göring against Ribbentrop, and Ribbentrop against Göring. Forgetful of Mussolini's presence, they raged at each other until Hitler rose like some star actor in a moment of climax and quelled them into silence with his towering wrath. His eyes were starting with anger. 'I will crush and destroy the criminals who have dared to oppose themselves to Providence and to me,' he raged. 'These traitors to their own people deserve ignominious death, and this is what they shall have. This time the full price will be paid by all those who are involved, and by their families, and by all those who have helped them. This nest of vipers who have tried to sabotage the grandeur of my Germany will be exterminated once and for all.'

Mussolini was the only one to retain his dignity, perhaps because he had so little left to lose. He rose, made his farewell, and retired back to his train. He was never to see Hitler again. Within less than a year both of them would be dead.

115

*Left:* Relics of the assassination attempt: trousers of a victim displayed for the photographer. *Above:* Speidel (right), Rommel's Chief of Staff

At almost the same moment Fromm was rising from his chair to denounce his subordinate officers – Stauffenberg, his Chief of Staff, and Olbricht, his Chief of Supplies. Stauffenberg refused to be browbeaten. He told Fromm that he had been witness to the assassination in Rastenburg; Keitel was therefore lying. Then Olbricht cut in to say that the Valkyrie signals had been going out during the past hour and more – the code-signals, he reminded Fromm, for national unrest. Fromm was so enraged he pounded the desk with his fists, demanding to know the name of the man who had dared to send out the signals in his name and without his authorization. He was told, Colonel Mertz von Quirnheim. When Quirnheim was summoned he admitted at once what he had done. Fromm was

about to place him under arrest when Stauffenberg cut in and told the General that it was he himself who had done the deed at Rastenburg. 'I detonated the bomb during the conference at Hitler's headquarters,' he said. 'No one in that room could have survived.'

Fromm faced him out. 'The assassination has failed,' he roared. 'You must shoot yourself.' But when Fromm realized that he was facing an organized group of conspirators, he threatened them all with arrest. Olbricht said he could not arrest them, because it was they who were in power now, not he. 'It's we who are arresting you,' he declared.

Fromm made an obstinate show of resistance, but he was soon overpowered. When Haeften and Kleist pressed their pistols against his fat belly he gave in. He was removed and put under guard in his adjutant's office. Using Olbricht's private lavatory, Hoepner had changed into the uniform he had brought with him. He

**The German War Office in the Bendlerstrasse**

was duly informed he was now Commander-in-Chief of the Reserve Army. At the same time Himmler, preparing himself to leave for Berlin by plane, was asking Hitler for a written warrant authorizing him to assume the same command, which the Führer had conferred upon him a short while before. So that evening there were three men each of whom held himself to be the Commander-in-Chief of the Reserve Army. No one at Hitler's headquarters seemed to think it necessary to inform the War Ministry of the change of appointment which had been made by the man who was still master in Germany. Hoepner, however, a careful man like Himmler, knew the value of having things put down on paper. When Witsleben finally arrived at the Ministry in a sour temper at seven-thirty that evening, Hoepner obtained a similar warrant from his supposed Supreme Commander of his own assumed appointment. His name, as well as those of Witzleben and Beck, was now being used when issuing orders from the headquarters of the conspirators. Hoepner was so punctilious that he spent much of the rest of the evening worrying about the comfort of Fromm, his predecessor, confined in an adjutant's room; he ensured that he had adequate food and wine sent up to him. He would have done better to have ensured that Fromm was well guarded.

Fromm and his adjutant, Heinz Ludwig Bartram, another wounded man of the Reserve and whose leg had been amputated, knew of a second, unguarded door in the rear of the suite of rooms in which they were confined. Bartram therefore had limited freedom of access to the rest of the Ministry as soon as he learned the timing of the routine checks by the guard on his and Fromm's presence. Gisevius, who remained at the War Ministry after Helldorf had retired in sheer exasperation at the way things were going, chafed at the softness of treatment accorded to Fromm. Beck at one stage even considered letting him go home, provided he gave his word of honour not to act against the members of the *coup*. This degree of clemency, however, was abandoned.

Around 16.45 hours martial law had been proclaimed, and by now, between 17.30 and 18.00 hours, the avalanche of enquiries began to pour in, keeping Olbricht and Stauffenberg leaping from telephone to telephone to inform, encourage, and cajole the questioners, the waverers, the doubters as well as those inclined to oppose the new military regime. The 'office' of the *coup d'état* had been moved along the corridor to Fromm's rooms, they were more commodious and better equipped to deal with the emergency, since many of the outside telephone calls were still being addressed to Fromm in person. Beck spoke personally to Stuelpnagel – the first direct contact the General had had with the conspirators that day, except for Stauffenberg's call earlier to Hofacker. Stuelpnagel assured Beck of his support, and then urged him to speak direct to Kluge at his headquarters in La Roche-Guyon, to which Blumentritt was on his way with the momentous news given him by Finckh.

In the midst of the busy scene at the Bendlerstrasse, SS Colonel Piffraeder arrived, accompanied by two SS men. He appeared to have no difficulty getting into the War Ministry. After clicking his heels and giving the Nazi salute, he asserted that on the orders of the Chief of Reich Security he must speak in private with Colonel Count von Stauffenberg. Gisevius feared this might be the herald of a Gestapo raid. He was the only one present who knew of Piffraeder's dangerous reputation, and he managed to warn Stauffenberg, who was quite prepared to meet these intruders with the same cheerful bravado with which he handled any form of opposition. However, he was wise enough to take with him Fritzsche, Kleist and Hammerstein,

and soon returned to tell Gisevius and the others he had placed the Gestapo men under arrest. According to Fritzsche, Piffraeder had sworn at them and behaved badly. 'Why not shoot them?' Gisevius had urged. But Stauffenberg was set on dealing with them later.

Gisevius's fears mounted. Where were the units who were supposed to have surrounded the administrative area long ago? Who was taking over the radio stations in the name of the new military government? Who had arrested, or better still assassinated, Goebbels, Kaltenbrunner, and Müller, the head of the Gestapo? No one seemed to know quite what was happening outside the charmed area of Fromm's and Olbricht's offices. Could not a small unit be formed here, in the Ministry itself, at least to deal with Goebbels and take over the principal radio station? Stauffenberg and Olbricht seemed to be too busy with their telephones to give attention to these basic matters. Nor did they seem to want to use Helldorf's men, since they were police and not soldiers. The *coup* was to remain as far as possible an Army affair. In the midst of all this discussion even a call from Keitel was momentarily neglected and lost. No one bothered to try to get him back on the line.

Another troublesome intruder was General von Kortzfleisch, District Commander in Berlin, who came in person to demand to know what was happening. He refused to see Hoepner when he was told he now occupied Fromm's place, and he refused to accept Beck's attempts at explanation. Words became heated, and he too had to join the growing number of men placed in detention. 'Don't you dare touch me,' he shouted at Hammerstein, who had been detailed to cope with him. This was an ill omen for the efficiency of the Valkyrie units on whom the conspirators depended, and which began to manifest themselves in the area around the Bendlerstrasse at six o'clock. They

included the Battalion of Guards commanded by Major Otto Ernst Remer (who happened to be an enthusiastic Nazi), certain units of the Army Fire Brigade Training Service and School of Army Ordnance, and units from the Infantry Training Schools at Doeberitz, the cavalry at Krampnitz, the artillery at Jüterborg and the Panzers at Wansdorf. Remer's superior was General von Haase, Commandant of Berlin, who was a sympathiser with the conspiracy. The orders given to these various units were specific enough. The problem lay rather in their willingness or ability to carry out these, to them, singular assignments under Haase's orders. Meanwhile Helldorf's men remained idle and unsummoned. The key responsibility of commandeering the radio stations remained unresolved. Though several of the units did indeed arrive in Berlin and take up their assigned positions, the business of the occupation in Berlin was conducted in a haphazard and ill-coordinated

**Hitler at Rastenburg on the afternoon of the Bomb Plot, (above) welcoming Mussolini, (right) showing himself to his staff**

manner. It was merely assumed by the conspirators that their orders would be carried out. But this was by no means the case on the spot. And similar ill-developed action arose out of the general confusion in the provinces. For example, in Hamburg the Gauleiter, Karl Kaufmann, told the author's colleague, Heinrich Fraenkel, how he and the Army District Commander, who was a friend, sat together during this summer evening joking about who should arrest whom as orders and counter-orders came in.

Remer, to take a key example, found himself charged with the responsibility of arresting Goebbels. Remer was deeply upset at the news of Hitler's death. He was the most efficient junior officer in the whole operation taking place outside the

Bendlerstrasse, just as Stuelpnagel in Paris was by far the most efficient member of the active Resistance – knowing exactly what action he was going to take against the SS and Gestapo in France and deploying the right number of trusted men to do it. But the conspirators in Berlin were to be faced now with their first formidable opponent – Goebbels himself.

Hitler had spoken to him on the telephone around five o'clock, warning him that some kind of military *putsch* appeared to be fermenting in Berlin, and that it was necessary to put out a broadcast to stop the rumours that he had been killed. He left it in Goebbels' hands to draft an appropriate announcement and organize its transmission. Before doing this, Goebbels summoned Speer, Hitler's young Minister of Armaments, to his house, where he decided to stay through the afternoon. He said that he wanted Speer's advice and help in this crisis,

but Speer believed the reason could well be that he wanted to keep an eye on him in case he too was involved in the conspiracy. Goebbels also telephoned the commander of the trustworthy Leibstandarte Adolf Hitler, the Führer's SS bodyguard stationed at Lichterfelde, five miles outside Berlin. He urged the commander to put his men on an alert.

Speer arrived at Goebbel's house, near the Brandenburg Gate, as soon as he could, and joined him in his office on the second floor. He found him conducting a spate of telephone calls, which must have rivalled in their intesity those taking place at the same time in the Bendlerstrasse. Goebbels' house, in fact, became the centre of the counter-movement designed to frustrate the *coup d'état* of which Hitler had warned him. Shortly after Speer arrived, the troops began to line up in the streets below; Speer drew Goebbels' attention to them. At the same

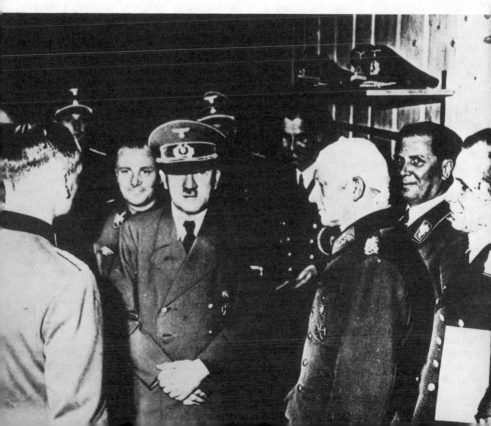

Admiral Dönitz, who quickly arrived at Rastenburg to reaffirm his loyalty

Colonel Quirnheim, leading conspirator at the Bendlerstrasse

time a writer called Hans Hagen, who acted as National Socialist adviser to the Guards and was Remer's adjutant, called at Goebbels' house, in order to warn him of the troop movements and advise him to speak to his friend Remer, whom he could trust as a loyal follower of Hitler. Hagen had been with Remer that very afternoon and both of them had been shocked when the Valkyrie alert had come through. It was Remer, in fact, who had sent Hagen to warn Goebbels in the first place, partly because Hagen was well known to the Minister, but also because he wanted to question the authenticity of the assertion that Hitler was dead. Goebbels agreed to see Remer at once, and Hagen was sent to fetch him. Hagen told Heinrich Fraenkel that the whole situation would have been changed for himself and Remer had Hitler been proven dead. They would then have obeyed the orders issued from the Bendlerstrasse, and arrested Goebbels.

Hagen could now be regarded as a counter-agent, spreading the news of Hitler's survival, which he had received from Goebbels, wherever he went on a borrowed motor-cycle in search of Remer. Haase, who on second

thoughts decided he no longer trusted Remer, had countermanded the order that he should be the officer in charge of Goebbels' arrest. Remer, however, was determined to see the Minister, who was speaking again to Hitler on the telephone, giving his excuses for not having yet put out the broadcast. Goebbels hastened now to draft the text with the information that Hitler had survived an attempt on his life.

The announcement went on the air finally at 18.45 hours, and was heard throughout Europe when broadcast on a powerful wavelength by the Deutschlandsender:

'Today an attempt was made on the Führer's life with explosives . . . The Führer himself suffered no injuries beyond light burns and bruises. He resumed his work immediately and, as scheduled, received the Duce for a lengthy discussion. Shortly after the attempt on the Führer's life, he was joined by the Reich Marshal.'

A transcript of this text was slipped into Kluge's desk at La Roche-Guyon at the very moment Beck was pleading with him to throw in his lot with the *coup d'état*. While listening to Beck, Kluge read the transcript. He then cut in with the demand:

*Above left:* Major Remer, Commander of the Berlin Guard Battalion. *Above right:* General Falkenhausen *Below:* Goebbels testing public opinion

'But what is the real position at the Führer's headquarters?' Beck was too honest a man to deny that things were uncertain at Rastenburg. This was too much for Kluge, who had spent years vacillating, and who was prepared to take no risks whatsoever. 'I must first of all discuss this with my officers, 'he said. 'Then I will call you back.' He promised he would let Beck know his decision,' but Beck knew with a man of Kluge's cautious temperament, this was tantamount to losing him.

The conspirators at the Bendlerstrasse had, of course, heard the broadcast. Though they had expected something of the sort to be announced, it renewed their anxiety. They immediately issued their official denial to the various commands with which they were in touch:

'The communiqué given out over the radio is incorrect. The Führer is dead. The measures already ordered are to be carried out with maximum speed.'

The telephones, like birds of prey, never ceased their assault on the men in the Bendlerstrasse following the broadcast that Hitler was alive. Beck, Stauffenberg and Olbricht continued to run from instrument to instrument either to issue orders, or in many cases to plead with field marshals, generals, or colonels who, in various moods of doubt and uncertainty, did not know what to do or what they should believe. Their voices hoarse, their energies over-taxed, the leaders of the Resistance were now at bay. The broadcast was a lie, they asserted. Keitel is behind it all. Goebbels is lying. Everyone but ourselves is lying.

It was plain, however, that whatever had happened to the Führer, the Nazi hierarchy survived intact and that the means of broadcasting remained firmly in their hands. The conspirators had only too much to explain. Hoepner was already on the way to losing his nerve. Even Olbricht was beginning to agree with Beck that Hitler might, after all, have survived in spite of Stauffenberg's continual reassurances to the contrary. The only heartening messages came from Stuelpnagel in Paris. When Witzleben had come, carrying his Field Marshal's baton, symbol in the conspiracy of the supreme military authority, they had had to face his wrath. Every one had risen, including Stauffenberg. The informal atmosphere was momentarily abandoned. Heels clicked. Witzleben refused to take any notice of anyone except Beck, who was the titular Regent of Germany and so superior even to himself in the house of cards the conspirators had set up. 'A fine mess, this is,' was Witzleben's comment. There was little Beck could say to reassure him. Down below, in the streets, the protective units were beginning to melt away, and the conspirators could do nothing to stop them. Some of their officers considered it was time for dinner. To rally support, Olbricht and Quirnheim had held an officers briefing session in the Ministry, but this only served to consolidate the opposition among the junior officers who were loyal to Hitler, whom they were now certain was still alive. Led by the Nazi enthusiasts, Colonel Franz Herber and Colonel Bode von der Heyde, they had remained on duty in order to initiate counter-action. They even complained bitterly to Delia Ziegler, who tried to calm them and keep them loyal to Olbricht.

Summoned by Hagen, Major Remer reached Goebbels's house. He still did not know whether Hitler was alive or not. The Minister for Propaganda received him at once, and demanded to know if he were absolutely loyal to the Führer. Remer reassured him that he was, without reservation. It was, Goebbels insisted, an historic moment. Hitler was alive, but the future of the Reich, he said, depended on this single junior officer. Goebbels was not Minister of Propaganda for nothing; he knew when to bring sentiment to bear. Speer watched him at work, turning Remer into his slave. 'We pressed each other's hands for a long time,' said Remer afterwards, 'and looked into each other's eyes.' It was like a play, with Remer an aspiring understudy who had suddenly been awarded the star part of his dreams. It was Major Remer, the Nazi David, the brave young officer with his Knight's Cross with Oak Leaves, pitted against those hideous Goliaths of subversion, Beck and Stauffenberg. Goebbels, to consolidate the effect he had created, reached for the telephone and asked quietly to be put through to the Führer. He had a direct line to Rastenburg. Remer stood there dumbfounded. 'Speak to the Führer yourself,' said Goebbels, handing him the receiver. Remer took it, tense with excitement. The hoarse, gruff voice was unmistakably that of the Führer.

Hitler also had a sense of occasion. He placed Remer under his own personal command, and ordered that he do his utmost to frustrate the wicked men who were seeking the destruction of the Reich. The safety of Berlin lay in Remer's hands, pending the arrival of Himmler, the new Commander-in-Chief. He ended by promoting Remer a Colonel on the spot. Hitler knew how to make a telephone communicate.

Remer, in a state of excitement and self-dedication, hurried out to muster what men he could for immediate counter-action. But by eight o'clock the opposition in the streets was already melting away. As darkness fell, Goebbels, with lights flooding the scene, gave one of his set-piece, highly professional orations to the small unit Remer paraded in the Minister's back garden. There was really nothing left for Remer to do.

Meanwhile, Kluge, exhausted by his tour of the battlefronts, sat back resting in the beautiful château of La Roche-Guyon, the seat of the Duc de la Roche-foucauld, whose family remained in residence in one section of their mansion, the rest of which had been requisitioned by the invaders. It was evening, and the dust and heat of the day were over. Kluge was a man who always felt his responsibilities keenly. He was sixty-two. He was deeply concerned, and more than a touch resentful, at what he had become involved in during the evening. These incriminating telephone calls from Beck alarmed him. Something very serious had happened, undoubtedly, at Rastenburg, but whatever it was must have gone sadly wrong. In addition to Beck's persistence on the telephone, he had received an anxious call from his friend General von Falkenhausen, who until recently had been in command in Belgium, and was another tacit supporter of a *coup* of some kind. Falkenhausen had wanted to know the truth about what was going on. With the Gestapo tapping the phones in Paris, Kluge did not welcome the amount of attention being paid him in this matter.

But worse was in store to disturb the quiet evening to which he had looked forward. Blumentritt had arrived by car around seven o'clock and brought one of the detailed orders sent out in the name of Witzleben before the latter's arrival at the Bendlerstrasse. It read:

'An irresponsible gang of the Party's leaders, men who have never been at the front, has tried to use the present situation to stab the hard-pressed Army in the back and seize power for its own ends. In this hour of deadly danger the Reich Government, so that law and order can be maintained, has proclaimed a state of military emergency...'

It went on to demand that Kluge arrest all the key SS officers and Party officials in the West. The mention of Witzleben stirred Kluge's weary spirits. Witzleben's name meant more to him even than that of Beck. Surely such men as these could not be wrong? He trusted them far more than he could ever trust Keitel. Perhaps Hitler was, after all, dead, as they said he was. But even as he was debating whether or not to issue orders for the arrests to be carried out, a signal was telephoned through

Hitler shows Mussolini, gaunt from his recent imprisonment, the results of the explosion

Otto Skorzeny the SS Commando
leader who sprang Mussolini from
captivity

from Keitel in Rastenburg asserting
that Hitler was alive and active, that
Himmler was the new Commander-in-
Chief of the Reserve Army, and that
any orders issued in the name of
Fromm, Witzleben or Hoepner were
invalid and countermanded. Authority now lay with Keitel and Himmler,
acting on the Führer's behalf. Kluge
realized what a good thing it was he
had not taken any precipitate action
in support of the *coup*. He realized yet
again how necessary it was to ascer-
tain the facts, and make searching
enquiries. He told Blumentritt to
telephone Rastenburg. But no-one in
authority was available; a conference
of senior officers was in progress.
Finally he managed to speak to Stieff,
whom he knew quite well. But Stieff
had long ago withdrawn his support
for any further action, since in his
view the attempt had failed before it
had begun. He did no more than assure
Kluge that Hitler was alive and that
the report on the radio was quite true.
He was careful in no way to implicate
himself or any of the others in what
had happened. Kluge rang off, utterly
disheartened. 'The bloody thing's misfired,' was his private comment. Like
Stieff, he was only for action if Hitler

were dead. But he wished the *coup* had
succeeded, for he knew better than
most how badly the war was going for
Germany.

But this by no means finished the
action in Paris. Stuelpnagel, who did
not accept the orders from Keitel and
had given his word to Beck he would
proceed whether Hitler were alive or
dead, was on his way to convince
Kluge, as his commanding officer,
that he should confirm the actions
already taking place without his
knowledge in Paris. To add weight
to his pleas, Stuelpnagel was bringing
certain of his most loyal and intimate
colleagues with him to La Roche-
Guyon. It was, in effect, a deputation
which was to visit Kluge as the summer sun was fading.

Stuelpnagel had with him Colonel
Hofacker (who was an experienced
advocate) and Dr Max Horst, General
Speidel's brother-in-law. It was approaching dusk as the car passed
through the gates of Kluge's château.
Kluge received them courteously in
the beautiful room he used for staff
conferences, normally decorated with
ornate tapestries which had been
stored away in case of war damage. It
all seemed most elegant and civilised
for so desperate a moment in the
affairs of Germany, though the ele-
gance seemed sombre and melancholy.
Kluge invited Blumentritt to join the
conference, and they sat down to
debate all the issues involved in this
troublesome business. Hofacker, because of his deep conviction and his
advocate's eloquence, as well as the
fact that he was Stauffenberg's
cousin, had been chosen to assemble
the facts and present the case to
Kluge. Hofacker spoke earnestly about
the need to liberate Germany from
Hitler. Kluge listened quietly and
seriously to a speech which appears
to have lasted uninterrupted for a
quarter of an hour.

It was almost dark in the grounds
outside the tall windows. Kluge said
nothing, though he was always prepared to listen, as he had listened so

often over the years to Beck and Tresckow. No one could say he was unreasonable, even though his mind in this case was firmly made up. Hitler, he was now sure, was alive. Hofacker went on, emphasizing the importance of the conspiracy in France, and its reflex in Berlin. Kluge was reminded he was master in the West. Germany, therefore, looked to him for the same lead Beck was giving in Berlin.

Hofacker stopped speaking, and everyone waited for Kluge's response. He got up.

'Gentlemen,' he said. 'It's misfired.'

Stuelpnagel enquired anxiously whether Kluge had known anything in advance of what was to take place.

'Certainly not,' said Kluge. 'I had no idea whatsoever.'

Stuelpnagel realized, as Beck had done before him, that Kluge was lost to the cause, and that he himself was therefore in a situation which could easily cost him his life. Already in Paris the men under his command were rounding up the key officers of the SS and Gestapo and placing them in confinement. He had depended on Kluge's acceptance of this *fait accompli;* he had, after all, been assured the *coup d'état* was under way in Germany. He got up and, without thinking what he was doing, went through the french windows onto the terrace, deep in thought.

..Then he heard Kluge's voice recalling him.

'Gentlemen,' said Kluge, 'will you dine with me?'

In the Bendlerstrasse there was nothing more they could do but listen to the radio they had not captured. An orchestra was booming out Wagner. Intermittently, it was announced that Hitler would be speaking to the nation at some time during the night. By now, the forces of the Third Reich were in action; the SS even went so far as to take Otto Skorzeny (the commando officer who had led the unit which had rescued Mussolini and brought him from Italy) off the sleep-

Albert Speer, Hitler's Armaments Minister, personal architect and intimate of his circle

ing car in which he was travelling to Vienna, so that his expert services could be available to counter the fading forces of insurrection. He returned to take charge of the final dispersal of any troops or tanks which might still be lurking in Berlin at the orders of the conspirators. When Himmler arrived from Rastenburg (only after midnight, according to Speer, who was still with Goebbels) he took care to avoid the Benderstrasse, although it was technically the headquarters of his new command. He preferred to join Goebbels and set up a centre of investigation into the abortive *coup* at Goebbels's own house. It was, he argued, much more effective conducted from there. But it left Fromm free to carry out his own vendetta in the Bendlerstrasse.

Dinner at La Roche-Guyon was a formal affair by candlelight. Kluge played the part of host with apparent equanimity. Speidel, who was present for a while, was called away on some urgent matter. Eventually Stuelpnagel's innate sense of honesty demanded that he tell Kluge the truth. He asked, while they were still at table, if he could have a word with him in private. They withdrew to a nearby room.

A few minutes later Kluge emerged in an unusual state of anger, shouting for Blumentritt, who was still sitting at the dinner-table. He was incensed by Stuelpnagel's insubordination, by the arrests of the SS and the Gestapo officers. The worst possible things were being done without any reference to himself, the Commander-in-Chief. He ordered Blumentritt personally to undo what Stuelpnagel had ordered to be done, now, immediately, before further harm was accomplished.

'Otherwise I shan't be responsible for anything, anything, anything at all,' he cried, his voice confused with anger.

Blumentritt telephoned Paris, and came back with the answer Kluge most dreaded. The arrests were already taking place. They had begun soon after ten o'clock.

Kluge was stupified. He turned on Stuelpnagel, who was a man he had always liked.

'Why didn't you telephone me?', he demanded.

'I couldn't reach you, sir,' said Stuelpnagel.

Kluge calmed himself, and sat down at the table. He ate and drank in silence. Then he rose, and the candles were snuffed. As they left the dining room, he turned to Stuelpnagel.

'You must go back to Paris. You must release those men. The responsibility is yours,' he said.

'The events have spoken, Herr Field Marshal,' replied Stuelpnagel. 'We cannot go back now.'

'If only that swine were dead,' Kluge said sadly, as he led Stuelpnagel down to his car. 'You must consider yourself suspended from duty. You had better just disappear.'

Stuelpnagel saluted. Kluge merely bowed, turned round and returned to the château. He realized what the night's events would mean for him.

In Paris, as in Berlin, events were to become confused as orders and counter-orders were received. Some 1,200 key officers of the SS and Gestapo had been rounded up with exemplary efficiency. Not a shot had been fired.

In the Bendlerstrasse itself despair had set in. With the departure of the units which had been supposed to support the revolt, the conspirators were left by themselves. By ten-thirty Olbricht realised the adherents of the *coup* were completely isolated, and would have to make a stand. In the War Ministry, those officers loyal to Hitler had taken their own line of resistance. Herber openly questioned Olbricht's authority; his associates, meantime, had managed to smuggle in some arms from an arsenal nearby. They were determined to liberate Fromm.

It was at ten-fifty that Herber, von der Heyde and their supporters launched an armed raid on the conspirators' headquarters. They broke first into Olbricht's room, when he was in conference with certain civilian friends of the conspiracy who had joined him that evening – Eugen Gerstenmaier, Peter Yorck, and Stauffenberg's brother, Berthold. (Otto John, another civilian helper who had been for some while at the Bendlerstrasse, had, fortunately for him, left on business connected with the conspiracy shortly before nine o'clock.)

Pointing his gun at Olbricht, Heyde challenged him that actions disloyal to the Führer were taking place, and demanded to be taken to General Fromm. Olbricht merely referred the intruders to Hoepner, whom he declared to be their commander-in-chief. Delia Ziegler, meanwhile, had run down the corridor to warn Beck and Hoepner, who were secluded in Fromm's room. On the way she met Stauffenberg and Haeften, who rushed immediately to Olbricht's assistance. They were met by gunfire and driven back into the corridor. Stauffenberg was badly wounded in his left (and only remaining) arm.

Firing then broke out in the corridor as a brief, pitched battle developed between the men loyal to the conspiracy and the men loyal to Hitler. Beck, Hoepner, Olbricht, Stauffenberg and Haeften were rounded up, but a few of the less prominent members of the staff of the *coup* managed to escape from the building. The rest were confined under guard.

Fromm, released by the Hitler loyalists, enjoyed his final hour of revenge. He was, of course, unaware that he had been displaced from his command. He set up a summary court martial around eleven o'clock. He was anxious to prove that he had played no part in the conspiracy against the Führer. Facing the leaders of the *coup,* he told them to lay down their arms. Beck immediately demanded his officer's right to keep his pistol in order (it was inferred) to shoot himself. Weary and unnerved, and bidding farewell to his friends with a final look in their direction, he failed with his first shot, merely grazing his temple. As Herber's men tried to wrest the pistol from his hand, he pleaded to be allowed to make a second attempt. Fromm agreed. He also agreed that Hoepner, who refused to kill himself, should be sent to prison pending an enquiry and subsequent court martial.

But he told the others curtly that if they had any last message to write to their wives, now was the time to get it done. Olbricht complied, and Hoepner also sat down to write. Fromm meantime set up a firing squad in the courtyard below, recruited from Remer's men. Beck, bleeding and almost helpless, was preparing himself for a second attempt on his life. Stauffenberg, who it was evident by now was badly wounded, had collapsed in a chair. He was bleeding profusely, and tended by Haeften. Fromm, his eye on the clock rather than on his victims, sentenced four of the conspirators to immediate execution –

Stauffenberg, Olbricht, Quirnheim and Haeften. Ten men waited below in the firing squad to execute them by the light of masked head lamps. Cars and vans had been hastily driven up for the purpose.

Beck revived himself sufficiently to try one more shot. He asked for help if he failed this time. Fromm agreed, and told a sergeant of the Guards to despatch him if the shot failed. It would seem that it did, and that Beck finally died as a result of a shot in the neck from the sergeant's gun. The others were led hastily down the stairs to the firing squad, Haeften supporting Stauffenberg, who was still bleeding and barely conscious. He revived momentarily as he faced the line of guns. The order to fire was given.

'Long live our sacred Germany,' he cried, as he died along with his friends in the volley of shots which rang out in the courtyard below Fromm's window.

As if in reprisal, the air-raid sirens were wailing over Berlin.

In the hotel Raphael, the officer's quarters in Paris, Stuelpnagel's immediate associates waited in despair for his return from La Roche-Guyon. The radio was on, with the repeated announcements that Hitler would speak during the night. They knew the *coup d'état* had failed and that the men they had been responsible for arresting must be released and, if possible, mollified. It seemed a hopeless position to be in. The 'black bastards', as the SS were called by the Army because of their black uniforms, would be able to take their toll as soon as their release was effective. Stuelpnagel's men drowned their misgivings in champagne. One of them, Colonel Linstow, who suffered from a heart condition, collapsed after having spoken to Stauffenberg on the telephone. Stauffenberg had told him that the forces of opposition were already gathering and would be upon them in the Bendlerstrasse at any moment.

Stuelpnagel arrived after midnight. There was nothing they could do for him but give him champagne and wait for Hitler's broadcast.

It came eventually at one o'clock in the morning of 21st July. The martial music hushed, and the harsh voice of the Führer, distorted almost to the point of incoherence by the after-effects of shock, ground out the words of vengeance which every man and woman sympathetic to the *coup d'état* most dreaded:

'A very small clique of ambitious, dishonourable and criminally stupid officers had formed a plot to remove me and at the same time overturn the High Command of the German armed forces. A bomb planted by Colonel Graf von Stauffenberg exploded two metres to my right. It very seriously wounded a number of faithful members of my staff. One of them has died. I myself am absolutely unhurt, except for very minor scratches, bruises and burns. I regard this as a confirmation of the decree of Providence that I should continue to pursue the goal of my life, as I have done up to now ...'

The surviving conspirators wondered if this could be the Führer. Or was it the voice of some actor coached to mimic the dead?

'The conspirators have very much deceived themselves. The allegation by these usurpers that I am no longer alive is contradicted by this very moment in which I speak to you, my dear comrades. The circle of the conspirators is a very small one. It has nothing in common with the spirit of the German armed forces and, above all, nothing in common with the German people. It is a very small gang of criminal elements who will now be ruthlessly exterminated ...'

It was, unmistakably, the obsessive voice of Hitler.

'I therefore now give orders that no civilian authority shall obey instructions from any office these usurpers seek to control; that no military authority, no officer or private soldier shall obey any orders from these men. On the contrary, it is everyone's duty to arrest, or, if he resists, to shoot at sight, anyone issuing or implementing such orders ...'

Goebbels, listening in Berlin, chafed at the ineptitude of Hitler's performance, the sheer paralysis of his delivery. Why must the Führer at such a crucial moment in their history neglect to use his professional services to help him draft and rehearse the broadcast? They were obviously in need of him at Rastenburg as well as in Berlin. He couldn't be in two places at once.

'To create order, I have appointed Reich Minister Himmler Commander of the Reserve Army ... I am convinced that with the disappearance of this very small clique of traitors and conspirators we are finally creating in the homeland the atmosphere which the fighters at the front need.'

Hitler's speech was being monitored by the world's broadcasting systems. It would be front page news everywhere, inside and outside the shrinking German empire, hard pressed on every frontier by the victorious American, British and Soviet armies. 'It is unthinkable that at the front hundreds of thousands, no millions, of good men should be giving their all while a small gang of ambitious and miserable creatures here at home tries perpetually to sabotage them. This time we are going to settle accounts with them in the way we National Socialists are used to doing ...'

The men on the run listened – Goerdeler in hiding, Otto John who was at home with his brother and the brother of Bonhoeffer expecting the Gestapo to call at any moment, Gisevius along with friends in their basement rooms in the suburbs of Berlin. Tresckow, far away on the Eastern front, had gone to bed in despair. Schlabrendorff brought him the news that Hitler was fulminating on the air. All Tresckow could say was, 'I shall shoot myself.'

'Probably only a few can imagine what fate would have befallen Germany if the plot had succeeded. I thank Providence and my Creator, but not because he has preserved me. My life

Hitler interviews the survivor Scherff, historical chronicler of the Führer conferences

is solely devoted to worry, to working for my people. I thank Him, rather, because He had made it possible for me to continue to shoulder these worries, and to pursue my work to the best of my abilities and according to my conscience . . .'

The men in prison could not hear this speech – the men already in confinement, Dohnanyi, Müller, Bonhoeffer, and others, and the men who had been hustled there barely an hour ago, among them Hoepner, Gerstenmaier, Peter Yorck, and Stauffenberg's brother, Berthold. Most of them lay in chains, huddled in the cells of the Gestapo, ready for the endless hours of interrogation. Hitler concluded:

'I may joyfully greet you once more, my old battle comrades . . . I see in this an omen from Providence that I must carry on my work and I shall therefore do so.'

The Bendlerstrasse in the small hours of Friday 21st July was floodlit by searchlights after the air-raid and guarded by the SS and Gestapo. Kaltenbrunner, Himmler's head of Reich Security, had arrived there in person before midnight, and his presence had prevented Fromm con-

tinuing with the executions of the men who had tried to involve him in the conspiracy. Still ignorant of his displacement by Hitler, he had sent out his own signal to the command he no longer held:

'The putsch attempted by irresponsible generals has been ruthlessly subdued. All the leaders have been shot. Orders issued by General Field Marshal von Witzleben, Colonel-General Hoepner, General Beck and General Olbricht are not to be obeyed. I have again assumed command after my temporary arrest by force of arms.'

When the SS set their guard over the Bendlerstrasse, Fromm realized it was time he left. He decided that he would call on Goebbels to give an account of himself, since he was uncertain to what extent he might be thought involved.

When he reached Goebbels's house, he was placed under arrest, once again. 'You've been in a damned hurry to get your witnesses below ground,' was all Goebbels said to him.

# Aftermath

**Freisler (centre), President of the People's Court, opens the trial of the Bomb Plot Conspirators**

The telephones were still at work at Goebbels' house during the early hours of Friday 21st July. One by one the suspects were either brought in or, like Fromm and Helldorf, came of their own accord in the hope that by reporting ostensibly to help with the investigations they might be held to have cleared themselves of implication in the conspiracy. Those arrested during the night included Haase, the Commandant of Berlin. Speer had watched Fromm try to persuade Goebbels to allow him to speak direct to Hitler on the telephone; instead Goebbels had merely placed him under arrest. According to Speer, Goebbels had always hated Fromm.

Goebbels was feeling triumphant, vain of the undoubted skill with which he had overcome this dangerous rebellion single-handed. When Himmler finally arrived from Rastenburg, Goebbels did not fail to rub this in. Himmler had taken care to be unavailable on the telephone during the night, flying to Berlin very late in the evening. He even avoided landing at Rangsdorf, arriving at an unspecified airport. He listened patiently while Goebbels poured scorn on the amateur methods of the conspirators. What fools they were to have left him, obviously their most dangerous enemy in Berlin, free to telephone Hitler, free to plan the countermoves entirely unmolested. Only Stauffenberg among the dissidents earned his admiration. Goebbels and Himmler parted at four o'clock in the morning, exchanging a handshake. 'The *putsch* is over,' said Goebbels, 'It's been like a thunderstorm. It's cleared the air.'

During the early hours of 21st July in Paris, the officers of the SS and Gestapo who had been rounded up and confined in the Hotel Continental, were all released. Stuelpnagel had held out for as long as he could, but finally yielded to the pressures of such men as Admiral Krancke, a Nazi supporter, who threatened to use marines to release these fellow-Germans if the Army would not do so. It was fortunate, in a way, that SS General Karl Oberg, the SS commander in Paris, was a former Army man. Stuelpnagel sent General Hans von Boineberg, the City Commandant who had been among those responsible for making the arrests, to invite Oberg to come to the Raphael for a drink after his release. Boineburg went to the Continental, thrust his monocle firmly in his eye, gave Oberg the full treatment of a Nazi salute, presented his compliments, told him he was free, and invited him to the Raphael to celebrate. Oberg, with a tricky situation to investigate, accepted – though naturally enough he demanded an explanation. When they reached the Raphael, Stuelpnagel sought to pacify him by telling him the arrests had been carried out for protective purposes because of the threatened Army *coup* – the SS, Gestapo and officers might well have been murdered. Whether Oberg believed this or not, he accepted Stuelpnagel's champagne and even shook him by the hand. For an officer of the SS, he was to prove a relatively considerate investigator.

Blumentritt, on Kluge's orders, arrived from La Roche-Guyon at three o'clock in the morning to take over Stuelpnagel's command. He was surprised, to say the least, to be invited immediately on his arrival to join the champagne party, and to discover Stuelpnagel and Oberg drinking together. As far as possible the officers of the Western Command were determined to cover up and live down the night's events as peacefully as they could. They were all Germans together in an occupied country, and must at least seem to show a united front.

Both Kluge and Stuelpnagel decided to take their own lives. Stuelpnagel left the champagne party to go to his office at the Majestic and destroy any papers which might be incriminating. His secretary, the Countess Podewils, found him there when she arrived at eight o'clock on Friday morning. At

nine he was summoned by Keitel to Berlin. He left by car after an early lunch. Late in the day, he ordered the driver to make a detour in the direction of Sedan, the site of the battle which in 1870 had decided the Franco-Prussian war. Here, where many officers and men of his regiment had died in their time, he walked away from the car and attempted to shoot himself – though for a while it was thought that he had been wounded by gunfire from partisans, who infested this part of the country. His floating body was dragged unconscious from the river, nearby, and he was rushed by his driver to the military hospital in Verdun. One of his eyes had been blown away by the bullet, which had penetrated his head near the right temple. After a hasty operation and a blood transfusion, he survived to stand trial with his fellow conspirators in Berlin later in the month.

Kluge tried initially to dissociate himself from the *coup d'état* by sending Hitler a full report of Stuelpnagel's actions on 20th July. This only served to make him suspect by both the Nazis and the supporters of the *coup*. Sick at heart, he began to feel that the whole blame for what had happened in France rested on his shoulders. Three weeks later the successor to his command, Field Marshal Walther Model, arrived from Germany carrying Kluge's formal dismissal in his hands; characteristically, Hitler had not even troubled to inform Kluge that he was expendable, and that he was wanted for interrogation in Germany. With the sound of the enemy guns drawing near to La Roche-Guyon, he left Germany on 18th August in a staff car. He took poison while eating his lunch under the shade of a tree.

When Tresckow, far away on the Eastern front, faced daylight on 21st July, he too determined to die. Schlabrendorff tried to dissuade him, urging him at least to wait and discover whether or not he was suspect. But life for Tresckow was now utterly without meaning. He ordered a car and was driven near the front line. Then he left the car and walked out into the no-man's-land between the German and Russian lines. Here he tried to represent that he was killed by Russian bullets; he fired some shots into the air, and then destroyed himself with a hand grenade.

It is most unlikely Tresckow would have been spared. Schlabrendorff remained at his post with quiet determination, waiting the inevitable summons. It did not come until 17th August. He was on the point of following his friend's example and shooting himself, but he says that a powerful impulse prevented him from doing so. He is the only front-rank conspirator, directly involved in one of the two principal attempts on Hitler's life, to have survived these terrible days. He was taken under guard to Gestapo headquarters in Berlin, the notorious prison on the Prinz Albrechtstrasse.

Of the other prominent members of the conspiracy, Fellgiebel and Stieff were placed early under arrest at Rastenburg, while in the days which followed the attempt, Hofacker and Finckh were among the first to be arrested and transported to Germany for trial. Witzleben, who was staying with his married daughter at the house of a friend some fifty miles from Berlin, had, we have seen, spent little enough time at the War Ministry, leaving when the outcome of the *coup* seemed hopeless and reaching the house again about ten o'clock on the night of 20th July. 'Tomorrow,' he said bitterly, 'the hangman will be here.' He was arrested at mid-day on 21st July. Goerdeler, on the other hand, who was on the run, had passed rapidly from refuge to refuge, staying initially at one or other of the houses of his many friends in Berlin, By 20th July he had left the city temporarily, though he returned again on the 25th. Since the Gestapo knew by now that

137

he was to have been Chancellor of the new Germany following the *coup*, the price of a million marks was placed on his head. He realized that he only brought danger to the friends who harboured him, and that it was inevitable he would one day be arrested. He finally left Berlin on 8th August on foot with a rucksack on his back, determined to set out to visit his family home in West Prussia. He reached Marienburg on 10th August, sleeping overnight in the waiting room of the railway station. He was wandering now in one of the areas where he was most liable to be known. He was finally recognized on 12th August by a woman in uniform who was familiar with his family, and arrested while trying to escape through some woodlands. Later this woman was bitterly to regret what she had done, and she barely touched the reward she was given by Hitler in person.

A very few of those closely associated with the conspiracy managed to escape. Of the younger officers involved at one time or another in the Bendlerstrasse, Fritzsche fled from the scene of the attempted *coup* and caught the last train home to Potsdam; Hammerstein also escaped, but had to go into hiding. Kleist, unfortunately, was arrested, while Delia Ziegler was subject to rigorous interrogation. Gisevius, whom the Gestapo wanted, lay hidden in Berlin in his civilian summer clothes throughout the winter, suffering severely from cold. He finally managed to cross the border into Switzerland the following January with the help of forged papers. Otto John, who was legal adviser to Lufthansa, calmly took the plane to Madrid on 24th July, leaving Germany without any difficulty.

On 22nd September a further bitter blow fell on the conspirators. Dohnanyi's secret safe at Zossen, still full of documents which would incriminate the conspirators, was opened by a locksmith in the presence of Sonderegger, the Gestapo investigator who had originally arrested Dohnanyi. These papers removed any doubt in Huppenkothen's mind concerning the guilt of the Abwehr group of conspirators, and those not already under arrest – in particular, Canaris and Oster – were quickly added to the distinguished group of men in solitary confinement at Prinz Albrechtstrasse, which finally included Goerdeler, Müller, Oster, Canaris, and Hassell, who was arrested by the Gestapo on 28th July. Other men close to the Abwehr circle, such as Schrader, preferred to shoot themselves.

Hitler was determined that ruthless interrogation should be followed as soon as possible by a series of show trials. Kaltenbrunner was in charge of the assembly of the evidence, while his large team of interrogators and officials (said at one stage to number as many as 400) was led by Huppenkothen. The vast body of documents behind the trials survived the war, and have come to be known as the Kaltenbrunner papers. Some 7,000 people in all are said to have been arrested and interrogated. The intensive period for the interrogations, which were conducted both by day and by night, was from late July to September, while the trials themselves, presided over by Roland Freisler, the notorious President of the People's Court, began on 7th August in the form of punitive and scornful acts of public vengeance on behalf of the Führer. Some two hundred at least are known to have been executed. Hitler was so appalled at the extent of the opposition to his rule which was uncovered, that he prohibited the presentation of much of the evidence in court.

The interrogations were conducted on varying levels of intimidation, following the carefully studied practice of the Gestapo. It was not normal in any case for the Gestapo to handle

**General Hellmuth Stieff, arraigned before the People's Court**

138

The face of defeat: Carl Goerdeler in the dock at the Bomb Plot trial

military cases, which were properly conducted by court martial. But the military among the prisoners had been stripped of their rank, and were to appear in court in ill-fitting and nondescript civilian clothes, their trousers unbraced in order that they might be deliberately humiliated. The trials, held under blazing lights, were both filmed and recorded in sound, initially for Hitler's private benefit, and film records of the executions were also made. The Gestapo could do what they liked with the prisoners, though those confined under military supervision in the Tegel prison, for example, were better off than those wholly in Gestapo hands behind the walls of the Prinz Albrecht-strasse. Some of the prisoners, notably Schlabrendorff, were tortured. Most were kept chained in their cells, starved, and left sleepless with their lights unextinguished. They were subject to constant and prolonged interrogation at any time of the day or night their captors chose.

The first to be arraigned on 7th and 8th August were Witzleben, Hoepner, Stieff, Haase and Peter Yorck, among others whose involvement in the conspiracy was fully established. Freisler was determined to make these trials the showpiece of his career. Like many Nazis he had a skeleton in his cupboard to make him more virulent; he had for a while been a Communist, before joining the Nazi party in 1925. He was a man of considerable, if limited intelligence; in court he used sarcasm and invective as his principal weapons of intimidation, seizing on any replies he could extract from his victims as an opportunity to pour scorn over them. Suddenly he would shout and scream with the cold-blooded, calculated rage of a sadistic school-master; he was like Goebbels, a professional, rather than a natural sadist.

Most of the defendants let their 'examination' pass with the minimum response possible; the more sensible among them soon realized during the first day that any response other than 'yes' or 'no' only gave Freisler an opening for attack. Witzleben and Hoepner, in particular, gave Freisler innumerable opportunities for sarcasm. Beck's housekeeper was dragged into the limelight to testify that his bed had often been wet with sweat during the period of the attempts in July. On the whole it was the intellectuals who fared best. Yorck's bluntness about the opposition to National Socialism proved a match for Freisler's invective, while a curious battle of wits amounting almost to an intellectual debate developed much later between Freisler and Moltke at the latter's trial, which was to come after long delay the following January. Moltke left his wife a detailed description of the trial in secret letters, in which he reveals a certain pleasure in his duel with Freisler.

The first phase of the trials led to the inevitable sentences of execution. The prisoners were in effect put on public display to receive Freisler's savage onslaughts, and then hustled away to be hanged in the Plötzensee prison, still under the fierce lights of the film cameras. One of the eye-witnesses to the executions described what happened:

'Imagine a room with a low ceiling and whitewashed walls. Below the ceiling a rail was fixed. From it hung six big hooks, like those butchers use to hang their meat. In one corner stood a movie camera. Reflectors cast a dazzling, blinding light . . . At the wall there was a small table with a bottle of cognac and glasses for the witnesses of the execution . . . The hangman wore a permanent leer, and made jokes unceasingly. The camera worked uninterruptedly, for Hitler wanted to see and hear how his enemies died . . . He had had the executioner come to him, and had personally arranged the details of the

**Tieless and handcuffed to a policeman, General Stieff is taken back to his cell**

procedure. 'I want them to be hanged, hung up like carcasses of meat.' Those were his words.

After similar trials, many of the remaining known supporters of the Resistance were put on exhibition and hanged – including Trott zu Soltz and Helldorf in August, Hassell in September, Hofacker in December, and Nebe much later, in March 1945. Rommel, as Hitler's most glamorous general whose guilt the Führer could not bear to have made public, was ordered to commit suicide as soon as he had sufficiently recovered from his wounds in order to do so. He died by his own hand on 14th October under the eyes of two generals sent to supervise his self-execution, and then for propaganda's sake he was given a state funeral on 18th October. 'His heart belonged to the Führer,' proclaimed Rundstedt during his funeral oration.

But it was not the Gestapo's way to lose hold of all their victims too soon. The more astute among the prisoners managed in one way or another to rouse the curiosity of their interrogators sufficiently to be kept alive. Goerdeler was one of these; though sentenced to death on 8th September, he developed his own technique of resistance within the prison, making long and involved statements in order to prolong the period of his questioning, and writing endless memoranda. At one stage he was actually employed by the 'intellectuals' of the SS to prescribe certain administrative improvements which could benefit the State under Nazism. All this he did, hoping to prolong his life until the war was over and he could be freed. Words and yet more words became his self-protection, until his interrogators must have finally seen through his devices, and he was suddenly executed in February shortly after Julius Leber and Count Moltke, both of whom were put to death in January.

More remarkable still was the case

of Dohnanyi. His method of gaining time had been to arrange with his wife for preparations infected with diphtheria germs to be sent him in prison. He hoped that by inducing chronic sickness he would at least be preserved from the worst effects of imprisonment and, above all, kept in military custody rather than moved into the clutches of the Gestapo. After the events of July he had been taken into the sick ward in Sachsenhausen concentration camp. The discovery of the Zossen documents, however, meant that Dohnanyi's feints and concealments, as well as his own attempts to win clemency through sickness, were of no further avail. In January 1945 he was moved to the Gestapo prison, where he suffered even worse neglect than he had received in the concentration camp. He was by now partially paralysed.

Dietrich Bonhoeffer had been confined in the Tegel jail at the time of the July attempt. In October he was moved to the Gestapo prison, Throughout his long confinement Bonhoeffer behaved in an exemplary way, radiating cheerfulness and faith in his Christian beliefs. His innate goodness commended him even to his interrogators and guards, and although he never wished it he came to be treated with a greater measure of leniency than the other prisoners. He endured the same state of starvation, which was their chief suffering. He was able to be of great comfort to his companions, especially to Dohnanyi, his brother-in-law, and to Müller, Canaris and Schlabrendorff.

Canaris had also learned the techniques of partial evasion under interrogation, and his presence proved to be a comfort to the others in confinement, owing to the keen sense he continued to possess for obtaining information. Like Goerdeler, his reactions to interrogation were to confuse and blind his captors with an excess of conflicting evidence which hurt nobody but demanded intensive research and prolonged cross-

Kaltenbrunner, whose security services found the victims for the treason trial

questioning, producing what one of his associates called 'an artistic distortion of the truth'.

Schlabrendorff received what was probably the worst treatment of any prisoner among those most intimately connected with the conspiracy. He was utterly unprotected at the Prinz Albrechtstrasse prison; he has written a full account of what took place. His chief interrogator was Commissioner Habecker of the Criminal Police. Schlabrendorff, with his disciplined mind and legal training, as well as his prolonged experience of living in a state of danger, perceived that Habacker knew far less about his activities that he claimed to do when he demanded instant confession. He knew the Gestapo's techniques, such as their use of forged documents or affidavits intended to force a prisoner's hand to sign a confession in the form they wanted. He denied everything, increasing their frustration with each refusal he made to implicate either himself or others.

*Above:* Freisler (right) and General Reinecke on the bench at the Bomb Plot trial. *Right:* Freisler conducted much of the prosecution case himself

So the Gestapo subjected him to torture. Like all the prisoners, he was in any case half starved, and chained hand and foot both day and night. When taken for interrogation, he would be subjected to long periods of waiting, and then suddenly faced with various interrogators who attempted to break down his resistance by alternating soothing and seemingly reasonable speech with sudden and savage outbursts of irrational invective. Habecker frequently struck him across the face when he was manacled and encouraged a young girl, who appeared to be his secretary, to hit him also and spit in his face. Schlabrendorff kept calm, as if expecting treatment such as this from people such as them, while quietly reminding them that their actions were illegal.

**Above:** Count Peter Yorck von Wartenburg. **Below:** General Witzleben like the other accused, was deprived of his belt even in court

**Above:** Hitler was determined to make Witzleben, the principal army defendant, a figure of ridicule. **Below:** Hoepner, stripped of his general's uniform, faces Nazi justice

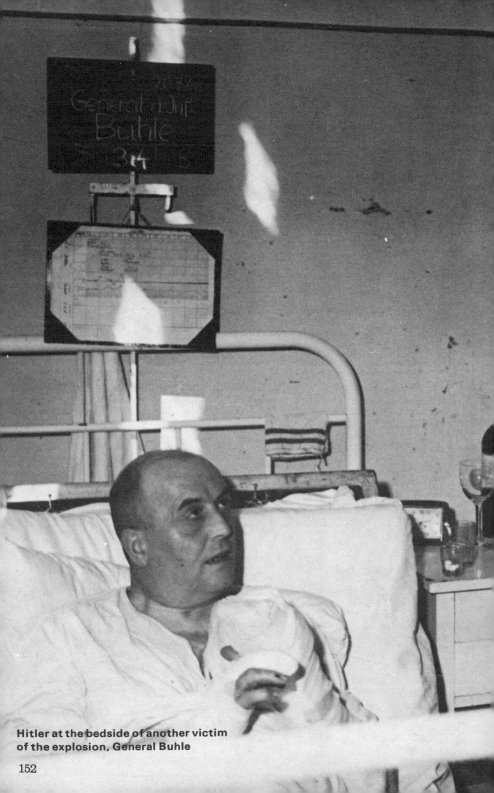

**Hitler at the bedside of another victim of the explosion, General Buhle**

Such behaviour did not rank in Gestapo eyes as torture. So one night Habecker ordered him to be tortured, a process carefully watched by the girl. His arms were chained behind his back, and screws were attached to his hands which drove spikes into his fingertips. When this proved ineffective, he was strapped down on a bedframe with his head wrapped in a blanket while another form of torture-equipment injected spikes into his legs and thighs. This, too, he managed to nerve himself to endure. Next, he was strapped in a medieval manner to a frame designed to stretch his body either with sudden jerks or by a gradual process of pulling. Finally, his body was trussed in a confined position; he was then beaten about the room with clubs, so that his face and head were badly bruised. When he was reduced to a state of insensibility, he would be dragged back to his cell and thrown on his bed, soaked in blood. After one of these sessions of torture he suffered a heart attack. He

was not the only prisoner to be treated in this way. As he says:,
We all made the discovery that a man can endure far more pain that he would have deemed possible. Those of us who had never learned to pray did so now, and found that prayer, and only prayer, can bring comfort in such terrible straits, and that it gives a more than human endurance. We learned also that the prayers of our friends and relatives could transmit currents of strength to us.

Only when he was threatened with worse treatment still did Schlabrendorff begin to contemplate suicide. Then the idea occurred to him to make a sudden, seemingly dramatic confession involving his dead friend Tresckow in plans for an attempt, not to kill Hitler but to persuade him to resign from conduct of the war. The Gestapo were delighted with this information, because it showed them they had after all been working on the right lines. It justified all their time-consuming efforts. Schlabren-

*Above left:* Count Helmuth von Moltke, leader of the Kreisau resistance circle.
*Above:* Hooks from which Generals Witzleben, Hoepner and Hase were strangled.
*Below:* The gallows house, in which many of the conspirators were executed at Plötzensee

Rommel's body brought by gun-carriage
to Ulm Cathedral for the State Funeral
which Hitler ordered

dorff was not to be tortured again – merely formally dismissed from the Army and held in confinement pending trial, which was not to take place until December. He sensed that the evidence the Gestapo had against him was still very slight; he was chiefly useful to them for the information he was thought still to possess. The Gestapo, however, had one further macabre trick to play upon him. He was taken by car to Sachsenhausen camp, and shown the execution site in the camp as a demonstration of what was in store for him. He was then taken to the crematorium and placed in front of the coffin in which Tresckow's body had lain since the summer. It had been exhumed, and was opened before his eyes. A full confession was demanded of him before his friend's body was cremated. Schlabrendorff refused to speak.

Late in December he appeared for the first time in the People's Court, but his case was postponed. He was, however, able to study Freisler's methods of examination. On 3rd February he was called again; Ewald von Kleist's case preceded his own. Kleist declared before Freisler that he considered opposition to Hitler 'the will of God'. Suddenly the air-raid sirens sounded; the Allied bombers arrived in great waves to bring Berlin the heaviest raid it had so far endured. The court immediately broke up; Schlabrendorff was fettered and taken to the air-raid shelter under guard. A bomb struck the court-room, and a heavy beam fell on Freisler just as he was leaving to take shelter. He was killed, and the file he carried representing the case against Schlabrendorff was destroyed. The Gestapo headquarters and prison was also struck. During the raid Bonnoeffer had managed to slip unobserved into Dohnanyi's cell, where he lay seriously ill and cruelly neglected. A few days later, on 7th February, Bonhoeffer and Müller were removed to Buchenwald concentration camp, while Canaris, Oster, Schacht, Halder and others were taken to Flossenbürg concentration camp.

Schlabrendorff's trial finally took place on 16th March 1945. With Freisler gone and defeat staring Germany in the face, Schlabrendorff decided to put up a vigorous defence, claiming that torture had been abolished in Prussia two centuries before. In his weakened state, the recollection of his sufferings broke his composure, and he wept in court. He was acquitted, but he knew far too much to be released.

He was eventually to be removed from the damaged Gestapo building. Late in March he was taken to the camp at Flossenbürg, where he believed he would be executed. Each morning at six o'clock prisoners were led naked to their execution, men and women alike.

Flossenbürg was to become the final centre to which most of the prisoners who in the eyes of the Nazis represented resistance were to be brought. The friends of the Abwehr died here together, as a group, following a summary court martial held by Huppenkothen in the camp laundry on 10th April. The war was almost over, and the thunder of the guns which represented liberation could be heard nearby. Bonhoeffer, Canaris, and Oster were taken out naked to be hanged before daylight.

Dohnanyi, who had been kept at the Prinz Albrechtstrasse building, had another short term under medical care in hospital. Then suddenly, early in April, he was taken on a stretcher to Sachsenhausen. Here he was finally condemned to death by Huppenkothen at a 'court martial' while still lying on his stretcher. He was hanged at Sachsenhausen on 9th April, the day before the execution of his closest friends.

Two days later, Schlabrendorff was transferred to Dachau. Others in the large group of distinguished prisoners

Niemöller, a opponent of Nazism who survived internment after the Bomb Plot

among whom he now found himself were Müller, Pastor Niemöller, and the families of Stauffenberg, Goerdeler, Tresckow and Hofacker.

After further transfer from camp to camp as the armies of liberation approached, Schlabrendorff, Müller and the others were finally liberated by the Americans on 4th May 1945.

Only Schlabrendorff and Müller of the original, inner circle of active resistance workers therefore survived. Others closely associated with them, or with those who had died, shared their good fortune – Schacht, Ewald von Kleist, Hans Fritzsche, Ludwig von Hammerstein, Otto John, Eugen Gerstenmaier, Hans Bernd Gisevius, Delia Ziegler, and the officers who had once volunteered for a suicide mission to kill Hitler, Axel von den Bussche and Colonel von Gersdorff.

But the rest were all dead – among them, Beck, Canaris, Oster and Olbricht, Goerdeler and Hassell, Stuelpnagel and Stauffenberg, Tresckow and Trott. They had died with some 200 others for their attempt to save Europe and the world from Hitler. Count Peter Yorck wrote on behalf of each of them, the known and the unknown, in the farewell letter to his wife composed before his execution: 'I hope my death will be accepted as an atonement for all my sins, and as an expiatory sacrifice . . . By this sacrifice, our time's distance from God may be shortened by some small measure . . . We want to kindle the torch of life; a sea of flames surrounds us.'

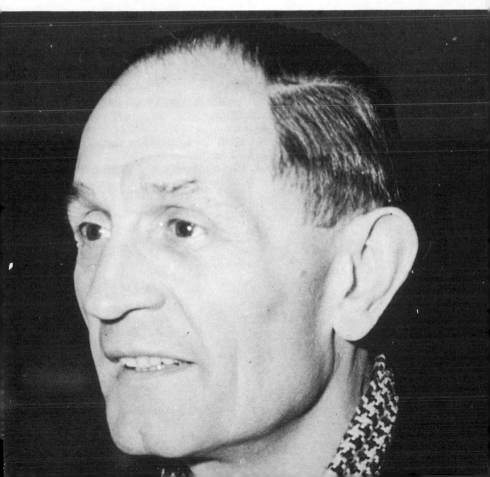

# Bibliography

*A German of the Resistance* by Count Helmuth von Moltke (Four Wells, Brunswick, Maine)
*The Secret War against Hitler* by Fabian von Schlabrendorff (Pitman, New York)
*Goebbels: the Man next to Hitler* by Rudolf Semmler (Loescher, London)
*Germany's Underground* by A W Dulles (Macmillan, New York)
*The Von Hassell Diaries* by Ulrich von Hassell (Hamilton, London)
*To the Bitter End* by H B Gisevius (J Cape, London)
*Germans against Hitler: 20th July 1944* by Hans Royce (Berto Verlag, Bonn)